PRAISE FOR
WHEN YOUR FAMILY SAYS NO

"Most memoirs of people forced to flee their families come from a place of anger and regret, but Laya's story begins and ends with love. Love separated her from her family, love brought her a new family, and ultimately, love created this book. That love shines through on every page, infusing even the most harrowing of events with hope. This is no small achievement, and it makes *When Your Family Says No* a haunting and powerful read by an author who truly has something meaningful to say about following your heart when doing so means giving up everything you've ever known."

—Diana Holquist,
Author of *Battle Hymn of the Tiger Daughter*

"A page-turning story of love and betrayal, *"When Your Family Says No"* gives us a glimpse into what it is like to live in the secret world of religious orthodoxy where every movement and thought is controlled and governed. Laya Martinez's voice is both tender and gripping. And, while her story has the power to break your heart, its greatest power lies in showing the reader that true grace and unconditional love arrive only when one has the strength to follow her own convictions. Don't miss this memoir, it could change your life."

—Suzanne Kingsbury, critically acclaimed author
of *The Summer Fletcher Greel Loved Me*

"*When Your Family Says No*" is Laya Martinez's own story of forbidden love, family rejection, and survival. It is an inspiring tale that offers hope to anyone who has suffered the pain of being disowned. Laya confides her innermost fears and agonizing dilemmas with honesty and heartfelt emotion. Her uplifting story will touch and amuse but also challenge us to reflect with her on the power of close-minded religious fervor to ostracize individuals and destroy families."

—Isabelle Gundaker,
Assistant Professor of Writing, Rowan University

"Her strict orthodox family, or love—which one will prevail? Which one should? A daily prayer for putting your right arm in a sleeve, a different prayer for the left, for brushing teeth—centuries-old mandatory and beautiful prayers learned from the cradle. Laya Martinez's life path was circumscribed with her first breath. And then she fell in love with a Gentile man. *When Your Family Says No* gives a rare and fascinating portrayal of life in the Orthodox community and tells of one woman's gripping and courageous journey to create her own life, a quest that is sure to be an inspiration to many."

—Carol Schaefer, Author, *The Other Mother*
(Soho Press, 1991)

WHEN YOUR FAMILY SAYS NO

A Memoir

- HOW ONE WOMAN FLED HER POWERFUL,
ULTRA-ORTHODOX FAMILY AND BUILT
A LIFE OF LOVE AND FREEDOM.

Cover Design by Agnieszka Stachowicz
Back Cover Photo by Amanda Stevenson
Internal Design by Julie Csizmadia
Website Design by: makeyourmarkdigital.com

Photograph credits appear at the end of the book and on the e-books

A Hebrew Glossary has been placed at the end of the book for your reference.

ISBN Paperback: 978-0-578-59216-9
ISBN E-Book: 978-0-578-59217-6

Published by Laya Martinez
P.O. Box 960, Narbeth, PA 19072
www.AuthorLaya.com

First Edition

Dedicated to Humanity

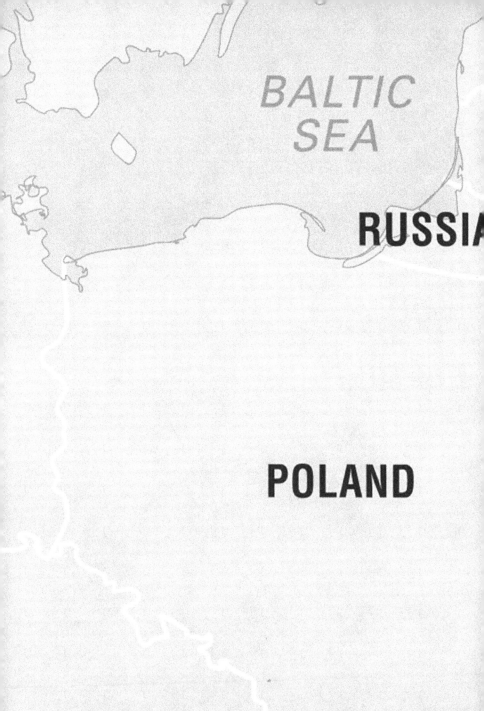

BALTIC
SEA

RUSSIA

POLAND

SLOVAKIA

LATVIA

LITHUANIA

⊛ **BELARUS**
SLONIM

UKRAINE

In the middle of the 19th-century Avrakham ben Izkhaak (1804 – 1883) founded a new sect of Hasidism and started the dynasty of *tzaddiks Slonim* (righteous men of Slonim). He created the Slonimer Yeshivah, which became one of the most influential in Lithuania and Belarus.

The Great Synagogue in Slonim
(Photo attributed I, Unomano)

Most of the names and places and some minor identifying details have been changed to protect the privacy of individuals. All the people in the book are real and the events described actually took place. The events were written from memory, and, when available, from Laya's personal journals.

A Hebrew glossary has been placed at the end of the book for your Reference.

"Here in Anatevka, we have traditions for everything: how to sleep, how to eat...how to work...how to wear clothes... You may ask, "How did this tradition get started?" I'll tell you! ...I don't know. But it's a tradition...and because of our traditions...every one of us knows who he is and what God expects him to do."

Tevye, Fiddler on the Roof

THE DAY BEFORE *YOM KIPPUR*, OUR MOST SACRED DAY OF the year, Mother woke us at four in the morning. "Come," she whispered solemnly. "It's time."

Despite the darkness and the fall chill in the air, my three sisters and I jumped out of bed like children racing downstairs on Christmas morning, our hearts pounding in anticipation. But we weren't about to discover presents under a sparkling tree brought by a jolly man with a list of nice children he rewarded with gifts. As Orthodox Jews, our reward came to us in heaven. This day celebrated the annual atonement ritual of *Kapparot*.

My mother led the way downstairs, my baby brother Asher in her arms. Candice, my oldest sister, had her rightful place directly behind my mother. Next came Marilyn, the middle child, who had made sure to squeeze herself between Candice and the second oldest sister, Syrle. I came down the stairs last.

"I'm scared," Syrle whispered in my ear.

Not me. I was four-and-a-half years younger, only eight, but ready to take on the world.

I squeezed her hand reassuringly as we proceeded toward the kitchen, the percussive chorus of clucking getting louder with each step. "Oh, Mommy!" I cried when we arrived, my eyes adjusting to the bright light. The normally quiet, clean kitchen had transformed into a boisterous mess. Five hens for the girls and three roosters for the boys squawked in their cramped, wooden crates. Newspapers covered the blue and white floor tiles.

"It's okay. It's the will of God," my otherwise fanatically tidy mother said, misinterpreting my thrill—*live chickens in the house!*—as horror at the mess and the wet manure smell of terrified fowl. My mother would do everything she thought God wished, even dirty her kitchen. In Biblical terms, she exemplified a true *Ay-shet Cha-yil*, a woman of valor.

The terror of the birds grew along with our excitement at being asleep one moment, then facing this lively ritual the next. My baby brother was cradled in my mother's arms. My other brother Mordechai, who had just turned five, hopped with excitement in his pale blue pajamas. My father, the patriarch, steered the show as always.

We would take turns according to age. My father opened the cage of the first hen. He wrapped a rope around its scaly, prehistoric legs, then turned toward Candice. "Grab it," he commanded.

She did. Then she swung. Then she chanted.

My anticipation and fear grew as my next sister, Syrle, took her turn. Then Marilyn.

Then came my turn. My father roped my chicken. "Grab the legs," he ordered. "Don't be afraid."

I grabbed. With his hands over mine, we hoisted the bird into the air, swinging it in big circles above my head. Feathers flew everywhere as I chanted in Hebrew, "This is my chicken! This is my sacrifice! It will go forth to its death and I will go forth to a good, long, and peaceful life!"

Lowering the chicken, I felt elated and proud. I had done it. I was blessed to live another year thanks to the grace of my sacrificial chicken.

After all six children had sentenced their respective chickens to death, my father swung Asher's chicken on his behalf, our cheeks flushed with accomplishment. The entire cast, family and fowl, waded through the ankle-deep chicken feathers blanketing the floor and marched outside to the waiting *shochet*, the ritual slaughterer my father had hired for the occasion. We all stood under the garage overhang, a hundred feet from the house.

With careful precision, the old man bent back the head of the first chicken, smoothed out the neck, pulled out his *hallaf*, a razor-sharp, polished knife used only for this purpose, and with one smooth motion slit the throat of the chicken and tossed it onto the lawn. The chicken, or what remained of it, ran and flapped around the lawn spurting blood madly until it eventually collapsed. This execution repeated the same way for the other seven chickens while we watched in utter fascination.

When the light dawned, my mother took the birds to the butcher to be feathered. She then brought them home to wash, brine, and prepare. She donated what we didn't need for our family to charity. The rest of the chickens would be consumed that evening at the feast that precedes the *Yom Kippur* fast.

I would learn later that *Kapparot* is not commanded in the Torah or the Talmud. The first mention in religious texts isn't until the ninth century, and even then, it remained on the fringe. But Kapparot is a quintessential Hasidic tradition. Like the social restrictions and the dress code, the ritual isn't based on anything biblical. This practice started thousands of years later in Europe. Many argue that it probably crept in from pagan religions and isn't a particularly Jewish thing to do at all. The people who consider themselves the "most" religious perform this ritual not because God directly commanded it, but because it's a visceral, active way to get close to God in the moment.

As I swung my chicken that day, I truly believed that my sins could be transferred to a doomed, squawking bird. I felt closer to God and my loving family. But at the same time, unwittingly, my father was teaching me the skills that would ultimately tear our family apart. Through this ritual, I was learning to act bravely and decisively based purely on faith. I was coming to understand that sometimes in life when the moment was just right and my fear was at its peak, I had to grab the chicken by its legs and swing, even if it made no rational sense, even if it went against everything normal in my world, even if I knew it would lead to chaos.

CHAPTER 1

SEVENTEEN YEARS LATER, I SAT ON A PLANE FROM NEW York to Reno, Nevada, staring at my reflection in the window, thinking about those magical, childhood Kapparot mornings. Just like on those mornings, it had become time to act. Just like on those mornings, I was consumed by excitement and determination. Only now, I was about to commit a sin so great, it would take a flock of chickens to cleanse.

Seven hours earlier, I had left everything in this world I had ever called home with a wordless goodbye. If everything went according to plan, I could never return. My family would not allow it. They did not see in shades of gray. For them, everything was black or white. In their eyes, I was about to go black. They did not traffic in equivocation or negotiation. You either have sinned or you have not sinned, and this sin was grave indeed.

The plane touched down in Reno, but it may as well have been Mars. As I descended the stairs to the tarmac, the hot, dry Nevada air felt suffocating after the New York winter I had left just hours before. Blindly following a line of passengers into the terminal, I became lost in a maze of slot machines, music, flashing lights, and Playboy bunnies.

I did not belong here. I was a twenty-five-year-old Orthodox Jewish woman with the face and experience of a sixteen-year-old schoolgirl. I still lived with my parents. I had never eaten in a non-kosher restaurant. I had only seen two movies in my entire life—*Bambi* and *The Sound of Music*.

Platinum blondes in sequined shirts towered over me on four-inch, spiked heels as they pushed past toward the casinos. I looked down on these women flaunting their bodies and wasting their money on gambling. But at the same time, this world swirled with excitement—the lights, the music, women walking with intent, men smoking cigars, winning and losing. This world was entirely foreign to me, its existence only hinted at in warnings about the slippery slopes of sin.

The mixture of contempt and exhilaration intoxicated me. I had no part of this world and never would. I had no desire to remove my prim hat and let my wavy hair swing down to my waist. I felt content in my high-neck blouse, conservative black jacket, and matching pencil skirt that skimmed my knees.

Unusual for a wedding dress.

But then, there was nothing usual about this day. I was about to marry a non-Jew.

> *You shall not intermarry with them; you shall not give your daughters to their sons…for they will turn your children away from following me, serving other gods; then the anger of the LORD will be kindled against you and He will quickly destroy you.* (Deuteronomy 7:3)

It was straightforward, direct, and absolute.
It allowed for no exceptions, no human emotion.
Like my father, my mother, my entire life.

So why was I doing this? Why, despite everything I knew and believed, was I about to risk everything to be with the man I loved? Better I murder a Christian than marry one. At least murder might have some plausible explanation: *self-defense*, maybe? But to marry one? Inexplicable.

I knew only one thing for sure: I couldn't stop myself. At that moment, twenty-five years old and inexperienced in the ways of the world, I truly believed that I was acting solely out of love. It would take decades to untangle the many strands of why and how I left everything I cherished in ruins. But now, I knew it was the time for action. I was a creature of faith. I had lived a life of being told not to ask questions or look for the rationale. *Faith. Love.* It all felt mysterious and preordained. All would be revealed in the end.

I descended the escalator of Terminal A, eagerly scanning the crowd for the love of my life. I would brave this strange, exhilarating, dangerous world for him.

"Laya!" John found me in the crowd. His eyes were soft and brown. His jaw was square. His neat, brown hair belied the military man he used to be. Instead of the *yarmulke* perched atop the head of every other man in my life, he wore a soft, felt fedora. I threw my bags down and let him sweep me up in his arms. It was our usual greeting, a grand display of love unlike any I had ever experienced in my serious and formal home.

He held me at arm's length to get a good look. His eyes scanned my straitlaced bun, my conservative clothes. But I could tell from the joy in his eyes that despite the restraint of my appearance, he saw only the intelligent, passionate woman longing for freedom whom he loved and for whom he had waited *six long years*. This may have been Reno, but ours was no casual, impromptu fling.

"I wasn't sure you'd come," he said.

"Of course, I came," I assured him. But we both knew it wasn't that simple.

Then his lips were on mine, and I melted into his strong arms. Warmth and security flooded through me, washing away my fear. Nothing else mattered.

"Finally!" I murmured, breathless at having him near again, my heart racing.

"We have our whole lives ahead of us," he whispered. He took my hand in his, and I gave myself over to the sweet relief that soon, all the sneaking and lying would be over. We would be husband and wife.

I loved skyscrapers, so he booked a room for us on the nineteenth floor of the tallest hotel in Reno. "What do you think of the view?" he asked, throwing open the curtains to expose the wide city below.

But I saw only him. "Perfect," I said.

There was no time to linger. We had to get to the Reno Justice of the Peace before it closed. Even though we had been secretly seeing each other for six years, without marriage we were frozen in place, stuck in a world of clandestine meetings and chastity.

"Did you send the telegram?" he asked as the cab rushed us to the courthouse.

"I did." Just hours before, when my plane had landed in Chicago, I had only twenty-seven minutes to catch my connection to Reno, but I had rushed to the Western Union telegram booth. The man behind the counter smiled warmly as if I had all the time in the world, as if what I was about to do would not change everything forever.

"How do I send a telegram?" I asked.

He explained, and I filled in the form: *I will not be home tonight, letter to follow, Laya.* If I hadn't sent word to my parents that I wouldn't be home, they would call the police, sure that something terrible had happened to me.

"That will be five-fifty please," the telegraph man said, his face blank.

I handed him the money and rushed to my gate.

Those ten words had been the point of no return.

"Do you have the letters?" John asked, pulling me back into the present.

I nodded. They were in my bag. If all went well, I would send them a special delivery as soon as we were married. If something went wrong—no. I refused to consider that option. What could possibly go wrong?

"Your family will never speak to you again. They will cut you out of their lives completely." His voice was low and tender. His eyes fixed on mine. We'd had this conversation a million times before, but now, it was real.

"I know."

"You're ready to do this? I love you more than life itself— but you must be sure."

I nodded again.

He held me gently against him as Reno sped past, a blur of neon lights and fantastic promises. *Lucky Jackpot. Fantastic Odds. Guaranteed Winners.* "I won't let anything happen to you," he said.

My fear evaporated. John was safety, security, everything to me. He gave me strength. I was willing to risk excommunication from everything and everyone else I loved for the sake of being with him.

Later, I would understand that not everyone has the privilege of experiencing the kind of all-encompassing love that we had found: intellectual, spiritual, and physical. I would also understand that not everyone had the strength of character to pursue love so pure and powerful, and face the consequences. At that moment, I didn't feel brave or unique. I didn't question the thoughts inside me that propelled me to act where most others acquiesced. All I knew was that life was meaningless without him.

I kissed his cheek, letting the warmth of him flow through me. There is a saying from Hillel, a Hebrew sage: *If I am not for myself, then who will be for me? And if I am only for myself, then what am I? And if not now, when?*

"If not now, when?" I whispered to my reflection in the cab window. My brown eyes stared back at me, resolute against the glittering backdrop of the passing city. I had always been a powerful person, never a shrinking violet or the type to second-guess. I may have been inexperienced, but not weak. I knew my mind and my heart. I wasn't running away from my family; I was running toward John—toward love. And if they couldn't understand that, there was nothing I could do but say goodbye.

PART I

In the beginning…

CHAPTER 2

A THOUSAND YEARS BEFORE I WAS BORN, A WOODEN FORT called Slonim appeared on the banks of the Schara River in what is now Belarus. Many flags flew above Slonim over the next five hundred years, as it was captured by each successive invading army, Russia, Poland, and Lithuania. Even the Mongols held it for a few brutal months. Then, in 1569, Slonim found itself under a Polish-Lithuanian alliance tolerant of Judaism. It became one of the very few safe places in Eastern Europe for Jews to practice their religion openly and run their businesses unharassed. The city flourished through the seventeen and eighteen hundreds and the community thrived.

Also booming at this time was Hasidic *Slonim* Judaism. It began as a reaction to the Reform Movement in general and to the Jewish Enlightenment in particular—a movement that pushed for a more secular, cultural, intellectual approach to Judaism. Hasidism is an ultra-religious, traditionalist sect based on the idea that serving the Almighty in happiness is the purest form of religious practice. Where traditional Judaism was more reflective, Hasidism encouraged active, present engagement with faith. Prayer, communal joy, optimism in the face of adversity, and the belief in the holiness of all things were given primacy over Torah study. Come dance in the streets for God!

The different schools or interpretations of Hasidism, are known as dynasties. They were often named after the town in which they started. Out of Slonim came Slonimer Hasidism. It was a more scholarly form of Hasidic Judaism, formed to shift the focus away from glorified mysticism and back toward the idea that studying the Talmud was the greatest good. It was a more pious intellectualism that stressed the importance of Torah study.

At the head of every dynasty is the *rebbe*. Unlike a Rabbi, who is respected in his particular congregation, the *rebbe* is a supreme leader revered by everyone in the community. No man would dare to marry, buy a house, or start a business without the *rebbe's* blessing. When a child is born, it is taken to the *rebbe* for a blessing. If a woman is barren, she goes to the *rebbe* for a blessing to become pregnant. He is a powerful and learned man, who is groomed from the age of thirteen for this role by his father, the current *rebbe*. A rebbe in training spends sixteen hours a day studying the Torah and the Talmud.

A rebbe does not have a business or trade, his business is overseeing the spiritual and day-to-day affairs of *his* community. A Slonimer *Rebbe* has a firm grasp on the understanding of human nature. He is always charismatic, with an ability to draw people in with his words, yet he is also strong and can be unyielding when circumstances are warranted.

He is a holy man who is regarded as the community's link to God himself.

I am the great-great-great-granddaughter of *Rebbe* Avraham, the founder of Slonim Hasidism and the first Slonimer *Rebbe*. This makes me Hasidic royalty.

Being the descendant of the founder of Slonim Hasidism made my marriage to a gentile even more of a betrayal. Not only had I broken with my immediate family and community, but with a historic line that reached back centuries.

Slonim Hasidism, like all Hasidic dynasties, believe that only they maintain and represent the original, pure form of Judaism. They had convinced many Jews that their extremely pious approach should be respected as not just a true connection to the past, but also as the best hope for the future of Judaism.

In reality, the opposite is true. The Reform Movement that Hasidic Judaism rejected holds the key to the survival of Judaism. Since the destruction of the Second Temple, Jews practiced their religion by studying Torah. Being able to read, understand, and discuss the Torah was a basic part of every Jew's life since childhood. This led them to develop a culture of learning, which allowed them to thrive in business and scholarship.

If being Jewish meant growing long beards and sidelocks and following oppressive rules as the ultra-religious would have it, I doubt the religion would have survived. Yet the rejection of secularization that took root in eighteenth-century Eastern Europe still exists. Today's Ultra-Orthodox, including my family, are among the most pious, literalist Jews to have ever lived.

Generation after generation my community joyfully marched backward over the abyss into a restrictive lifestyle that had nothing to do with the Torah and the Talmud, and I would spend most of my adult life trying to understand the appeal of Hasidic cultish insularism. Why had I dared leave it when the rest of my siblings had not? And what was my role now toward my community and the people I still dearly loved, even if they had renounced me?

I wasn't ignorant of what my family had survived to get where we were today. Beyond my specific ancestry, my identity, like that of all Jews, is forever tied to the attempted mass extinction of my race.

When the Nazis rolled into Slonim on June 24, 1941, more than 22,000 Jews lived within its walls. The Nazi-era Slonimer *rebbe*, my great-grandfather *Rebbe* Shlomo, had heard from the recent refugees the horrific stories of what the Nazis did to Jews. But he was a leader, and his responsibility was more than just to himself. He refused to leave his town and his people and would perish with them. Hundreds of Jewish men were rounded up, marched into the stadium, and beaten to death. The lucky ones were shot in the street. Jews were ordered out of their homes and into the Slonim ghetto, which they constructed through forced labor.

On July 17, 1941, the Einsatzgruppen arrived in Slonim. The Einsatzgruppen was the mobile killing squad of the Nazis. It was dispatched behind the advancing army to kill "undesirable" civilians, which included the intelligentsia, Soviet political commissars, Jews, gays, and gypsies. It rounded up its victims, shot them, and buried them in mass graves. Only after its methods were deemed "inefficient," both for the slow pace and the psychological toll it took on the officers, did the Nazis develop extermination camps. Of the six million Jews killed in the Holocaust, the Einsatzgruppen is estimated to have killed 1.3 million.

The morning they arrived in Slonim, the Einsatzgruppen surrounded the city and cast out 1,200 young men, telling them they were being sent to work. They were marched up a hill to burial pits and shot.

On the eve of November 14, 1941, the Einsatzgruppen did its second sweep of Slonim. Somewhere between 8,000 and 10,000 Jews were marched out of the ghetto, shot, and left for dead in mass graves. A few escaped from under the pile of bodies to go back to the Slonim ghetto to warn their friends and family. When the Nazis discovered these survivors, they were shot. Within three years, a thriving Jewish community that had endured almost five hundred years of war and destruction, that had flourished to become one of the most influential cultural, economic, and religious centers in Eastern Europe, was decimated.

Family lore tells of a prophet. He warned of the troubles that would befall Europe. The great *rebbe's response* was to send a single grandson to Turkish Palestine to set up a *yeshiva*. Had Noah Steinberg stayed in Slonim, my bloodline, like so many others, would have been erased from the earth.

At the start of the First World War my grandfather, one of Noah's descendants, ran a wheat mill on the Jordan River. The river current near the mill attracted fish, which in turn attracted young Arabs who sought to catch the fish to feed their hungry families, despite the posted signs warning of the danger the mill posed to those who came near. Eventually, a young woman got too close to the machinery and was severely disfigured. The Ottoman Turkish government jumped at the opportunity to wrest the mill from a Jew and punish him for disfiguring an Arab girl.

My frantic grandfather told my grandmother, "If the townspeople don't kill me before I go to jail, they'll kill me *in* jail." He knew a fair trial was not in the cards for a Jew.

"Ask the *rebbe*," my grandmother responded. "He'll know what to do."

"The war will last too long," the *Rebbe* told him. "Sail immediately for the United States."

"But I can't afford..."

"Send for your family when you can."

After my grandfather fled, my grandmother and their two young children continued to live in the small town of *Tzfat*, one of Judaism's Four Holy Cities, and the center of *Kabbalah* (the mystical branch of Judaism). They lived with her father who was a respected *rebbe*, and a poor one, as all rebbes were in those days. His house was small and made of stone, with a dirt floor and one wooden door at the front. It was wedged next to many other small stone houses on a narrow cobbled street in Northern Palestine. Most of the day, my five-year-old father was in *Cha'dar (Jewish kindergarten)*, praying and studying the Torah and Talmud beside long-bearded *rebbes*. When there was time to play, my father and his sister ran around camels' ankles and kicked stones in the street with the many other neighborhood children to amuse themselves.

My grandmother survived by making woolen stockings to sell in Syria. An ocean away, my grandfather worked night and day establishing his own small business on the Lower East Side of Manhattan selling buttons, yarn, and inexpensive trimmings.

In 1921, six years after his escape, he was finally able to send for his family.

After a trip on camelback to Egypt, a train to Rotterdam, and a trans-Atlantic voyage to Ellis Island, my father arrived in New York City, his eleven-year-old eyes wide with excitement and fear. He spent his American youth living in a nice apartment on the Lower East Side, attending a religious Jewish school, and continuing his Talmudic studies.

At twenty, he was sent away to study at a *yeshiva* seminary (Jewish college for boys) in Poland, a great honor. He was a brilliant scholar and loved his time there. But back in New York, my grandfather's business was struggling. He desperately needed his son's help, so my father dutifully returned to Manhattan. Within a decade, my father had turned the shop into a thriving enterprise and in the process became a very wealthy man.

When my grandfather died, my father supported his mother in luxury for the rest of her life. Perhaps he did this to compensate for the lack of love his mother had gotten from her husband.

At sixteen, my grandmother had been betrothed to a thirty-three-year-old man with two children. She was in love with a seventeen-year-old boy at the time, but that didn't matter. Her family was poor. Her father was an esteemed, learned man in the Talmud and would study in the *shtetl* 14 hours a day. This was deemed more important than anything wealth could afford. However, God sent no money from heaven. He needed nothing for himself, but what about his wife and daughter? My grandmother married not for love but for practical considerations. Within the year she bore my father.

Several years after my grandfather's death, another man wanted to propose to my grandmother. Finally, she might live the last years of her life with love after a lifetime of sacrifice. But my father would not hear of it, and as the male of the family, he was in charge of his mother. This new suitor, later to become the head Rabbi of Israel, was considered a step down in the eyes of my father because he wasn't part of a dynastic family. It was not to be.

I did not know my grandmother's full story at the time I eloped with John. When I learned about it later, it further confirmed what I had been raised to believe intrinsically: that my happiness, like my grandmother's, was secondary. At the time, I was so brainwashed that this made perfect sense. Who was I to demand happiness? But my grandmother's story also highlights another crucial point: it wasn't just that I must marry a Jew, but that I must marry the right *sort* of Jew. Thus, there was more at work in my situation than just shared responsibility to the Jewish race. I held a sacred duty to uphold my family's sense of self-importance. The shame of my leaving was not just religious or genealogical, it was sociological: we were royalty, and I had chosen a commoner.

My mother's family found their way from Europe under better circumstances than my father's. They came from Germany and Poland in 1849 in search of a new world without anti-Semitism in the social mobility of America. They were modern Orthodox Jews, observant of all religious laws, but much more integrated into secular society than Ultra-Orthodox Jews. At a young age, my grandfather founded an insurance company in Virginia, which became a success.

When it was time to settle down, my grandfather faced a significant demographic dilemma: there were almost no other Jews in Virginia. He had to travel over five hundred miles to South Carolina to find my grandmother. He was the lucky one. Six of his seven siblings were girls who never married because they could not, like their brothers, go out into the world and find Jewish mates. The stigma of spinsterhood was an acceptable fate. Marrying a non-Jew was unthinkable.

My maternal grandmother was Jewish but was completely secular and non-observant. All she knew of Judaism was that it was her religion, she believed in God, and she was not allowed to marry a non-Jew. The last point she knew from experience. Two of her brothers married non-Jewish women and they had been shut out of the family. No matter the variety of Jew, that was the one prohibition that always applied.

After a short period of proper introductions, stilted long-distance mating rituals, and a modest wedding, my grandfather brought his bride back to Virginia and taught her how to pray and read Hebrew. He taught her how to observe the Sabbath and the laws of being kosher. She loved every bit of it, while also accepting her new husband's rigid Germanic traditions. They were truly and fully in love with each other.

My grandparents started a family in Baltimore, quickly producing two beautiful, healthy children, my mother Sheila, and her older brother, Marvin. But their third baby was stillborn. Their next baby was born healthy, only to die in its crib a year later.

The family was devastated by the double loss. My uncle, the eldest child, took it the hardest. He settled into a deep depression. It was 1915, and enlightened ideas about accepting "mental illness" were not the norm. He was sent away to a home, developed an illness, and died at the age of 21.

My grandparents became maniacal about protecting my mother, their one remaining child. They guarded her with unnatural intensity. There were no locks on any doors, including the bathroom. The door to my mother's bedroom had to stay open all day and night so that my grandmother could see her child, safe and breathing. The atmosphere in their home was one of German strictness and constant vigilance. My mother grew up in a house full of adoration, but devoid of freedom. She was less a child than a survivor, a lone representative of lost hopes and dreams, and a carrier of great responsibility and survivor's guilt.

What did this mean when trying to understand my mother? She was not raised in an ultra-religious world yet came to believe wholeheartedly.

This story is as much the story of her moving backward as it is of me moving forward.

CHAPTER 3

M Y PARENTS WERE INTRODUCED THROUGH THE LOCAL matchmaker. My father was a successful and charismatic young man on his own merits, in addition to being part of a Hasidic Dynasty. This allowed him the luxury of high standards. He wanted, of course, a pious and respectable wife. Of utmost importance, she must have *yichus* (fine pedigree). Nothing could blemish the family name. My mother was a virtuous woman of faith with *yichus* aplenty. She had a degree from Hebrew College, a rare feat for a woman at the time, and was an accomplished tennis player. My mother was tall with blue eyes and blonde hair, unusual for her Jewish heritage. She was a fourth-generation American, from a family of concert pianists.

My father, Morton Steinberg, was born in Israel and had a Mediterranean complexion. He was broad-shouldered and very handsome. They looked like an everyday American couple; well-dressed but never wearing religion on their sleeves.

My father traveled every week from New York to Maryland to court my mother. He wrote her love letters that began, "My Chummy Sheila." She kept them in a box in her dresser her entire life. They married quickly and moved to the Orthodox community on the Lower East Side where my father ran his flourishing textile business. The family's history was following a familiar and expected track: Jews going to great lengths to marry Jews. This is what our people do, what our family does, and what our family has done since the beginning.

My father knew he did not want to raise his children in the bustling confines of the Lower East Side. He had grown up in a cramped stone house in a poor area of what was then Palestine. After his arrival in America, his family had moved into a Lower East Side tenement house with a tiny courtyard that teemed with the children of two hundred tenants. Now a rich man, he could fulfill his dream of a spacious home and a suburban lawn. His children would play outside on grass, breathing fresh air, accompanied only by the songs of the birds and the peals of their own laughter.

My father bought a house on the south shore of Long Island and moved the family there when my eldest sister Candice was born. My parents were pioneers, the first Jewish Orthodox family to live in Woodmere. They were sure the community would soon expand with new synagogues and families. My father knew how to build a community as surely as he had built his business. He founded our local synagogue as well as an Orthodox school for my brothers. Fifty years later, the school has 2,000 students.

Later, despite their success at creating a vibrant Orthodox community around us, my parents would beat themselves up over the decision to move in among non-Orthodox strangers. True, we lived a charmed childhood, running, biking, and playing baseball with the other children in the neighborhood. And as my father predicted, the area did become more Orthodox. But if we had been enmeshed in a religious neighborly community from the start, my parents later wondered, would I have never been tempted away?

When Candice was two years old my mother gave birth to my sister Syrle, then to my sister Marilyn two years after that. With each successive daughter, very real anxiety began to grow in my father: would he ever be blessed with a son? As with most heavily religious cultures, men outranked women in Orthodox Judaism. Boys study the Talmudic Bible to become great rabbis. They are the scions who uphold tradition and carry on the proud family name.

The Orthodox would tell you that the woman is at least as important as the man because she makes the man's life possible. She shapes his home and instills proper values into their children. But Orthodox girls did not study the Talmud. They went to school to learn how to be good Orthodox wives and mothers. Indeed, a man's great reward in the afterlife is based on the sum of his accomplishments. A woman's reward is based on the accomplishments of her husband.

I was the fourth daughter to arrive and they named me Rita Leah Steinberg. Given his culture, it was difficult for my father to have a fourth girl populating the family. In the Jewish culture, you are supposed to have a child of each sex and keep trying until you succeed. When I was born and the delivery nurse came out to announce my arrival, he replied, "Are you sure?"

It took three more prayer-filled years before God granted the Steinbergs a son, my brother Mordechai. Five years later, my last brother, Asher, would arrive to complete our family.

On the corner of two quiet streets in suburban Long Island sat a large two-story home. This was our home, detailed by a stone facade, surrounded by trimmed lawn, and lots of fragrant rose bushes in front that flanked the slate walkway to our door.

Even then, I knew our home to be impressive, inside and out. When you entered the house, you were greeted by a sweeping circular staircase and the winking sparkles from two matching crystal chandeliers, one upstairs and one down. The vestibule had a coat closet for men and a separate closet for women.

The living room and dining room were exquisitely decorated and formal, demanding the proper respect. We never played in those rooms, and only ate in the dining room on the Sabbath. All other meals were taken in the breakfast room or the kitchen, which was spacious enough to fit a table that accommodated the eight of us, plus all the cabinets needed to store two separate sets of dishes, flatware, and pots and pans. One set was used only for foods containing milk, and one set only for foods containing meat. There was a guest bedroom behind the kitchen where the help would stay.

The Steinberg household was bustling, and not only with six children. Everyone was welcome in our home. JFK Airport taxicab drivers knew the destination of the passengers who had traveled from Israel, and Jews arriving from anywhere always had a place at the Steinbergs', no reservations necessary. People came from all over the world and they were welcomed with a private room, a meal, and a smile.

My parents not only opened their home but also their wallets. They gave most of their extra time and money to Jewish projects and charities, some of which remain staples of the community today. Jewish beggars, called *meshulachim* (messengers of charity), knew that if they wanted money, ours was the house to visit. They would get off the train and walk to our door. When we'd hear the knock, we would run through the house calling, "A *meshulach*! A *meshulach*!" My parents made tea, offered a meal, and always gave money for food, weddings, school, holidays, whatever the men needed. But it wasn't the charity that most impressed me; it was that my parents always treated these men with the utmost respect.

Yet despite being pillars of the Orthodox community, my parents in no way resembled the modern image of Hasidic Jews. Even my father, a man who studied the Talmud in every moment of his free time, every day of his life, did not don a beard or an all-black suit. Nor did my mother wear a wig or restrict her closet to long, loose dresses. My father was a meticulous dresser and always looked sharp in his tailor-made business suits and an impeccably brushed felt hat, which he traded for a straw hat when warmer weather arrived. He kept his face close-shaven and gave no quarter to stray hairs.

My mother was fashionable and shopped at stores for the well-to-do. She wore slacks and a cropped leather jacket in winter, and short-sleeved tops in the summer. She never styled or even brushed her hair, but instead went to the beauty parlor where it was carefully arranged and then intensely hair sprayed to ensure that each of her lovely blond hairs would stay exactly in its place throughout the week. When my father was about to come home, she would apply lipstick, dabbing some on her finger to use as blush. She needed no other makeup to look pretty for her husband.

It was at the many galas and formal events they attended together, where my mom noticed other women with make-up. I decided I would do her makeup for the first time at the upcoming gala that Sunday evening. "On me?" She was so excited.

I put on brown mascara to cover her blond lashes, eye shadow, and lipstick. She loved it. She never bothered to take the time to do this for herself. It was a special time that we spent together, and I so much wanted to make her happy. She was delighted.

In their home and at the temple, they were devout in upholding the traditions and values of their ancestors. But in the outside world, they were eager to embrace American culture. They never felt that these two identities clashed.

Soon, that would all change.

CHAPTER 4

T HERE ARE 613 BIBLICAL LAWS IMPOSED ON THE JEWISH Nation, made up of 248 positive commandments and 365 laws containing what is forbidden.

The first rays of morning light shine through the curtains. Darkness still cloaks my sleeping brother and me in our twin beds as the birds have begun to sing outside, and our suburban town begins to wake.

A typical morning in our household would go something like this: mother energetically opened the door to each one of our rooms. With wide eyes and a sense of enormous cheer, she sang out loud to every one of my siblings and me, with a voice that rang through the halls of our home:

Az Kanamair	*Be strong like a tiger*
Kal Ka'nesher	*Swift like an eagle*
Rawtz Katzvie	*Run like a deer*
Giboar Ka'Ari	*Be strong like a lion*
La' A'sose ritzon avichah	*To do the will of your Father*
sheh ba'shamayim ooh va'aretz!!	*who is in Heaven and on Earth!!*

To this day, my mother's happy, off-tune voice still rings in my ear when I awake tired and don't want to get out of bed.

When I would finally open my eyes, I stretched to a sitting position and tiredly uttered the Morning Prayer, *Modeh Ani,* which begins: *I give thanks, living and enduring King, for You have graciously returned my soul within me. Great is Your faithfulness.*

For men, the morning blessings include praising God "for not making me a *gentile, a woman, or a slave.*"

I liked being female, so I always wondered why *my* prayer did not include, *"...who has not made me a man."* Why would God make a member of the human race a slave in the first place?

I slumped, still half asleep, into the bathroom. I took a cup of water in my right hand and poured it on my left hand, filled the cup with water again, and used my left hand to pour water on the right. This was repeated three times. There was no spoken blessing because you're not allowed to utter God's name in the bathroom. But, as soon as I left the bathroom, I stood near the door and whispered *Asher Yatzar*, thanking God for giving humans orifices and not blocking them up. *How else could we be born?*

> *Blessed are You, Lord our God, King of the universe, who fashioned man with wisdom and created within him many openings and many cavities. It is known before Your throne of glory, that if but one of them were to be ruptured, or one of them were to be blocked, it would be impossible to survive.*

My sister Syrle passed me in the hall. "Hurry!" She called to me as she raced down the stairs.

I ran back to my bedroom to dress for school. Several lines in Leviticus seem to give preference to the right side of the body so everything that went on my body, down to my socks and shoes, was always put on the right side of my body first, then the left. We honor the right side by attending to it first. When the clothing is removed, the left is removed first, then the right, which is seen as further honoring the right side. If any of my garments were new, I would recite the prayer for new clothes because I was experiencing the joy of a new garment.

The constant prayers and rituals of my childhood were both soothing and mind-numbing. I had been reciting these prayers since I could utter a sound. Like the natural rhythm of breathing, they were spoken automatically. I knew them so well that I didn't even have to think about them. For us, everything was about God. Every truth was in the Talmud. Every movement is dictated by law.

I remember huddling under the hallway table one day, six years old and guilty of a great crime. I shook with fear as my father's footsteps echoed up the front walk, lined by the rose bushes he loved so. His hard, black synagogue shoes sounded brisk, resonant, and somehow holy as they reverberated against the slate.

The heavy wood door swung open. A rush of cold air floated to my hiding spot, covering my already chilly body. I heard my father remove his hat and coat while in the vestibule. He hung his coat in the men's closet, took off his outside hat, and placed it on the ornate wood table. Every act was accompanied by the appropriate prayer. He walked into the hall where I cowered, whispering prayers under my breath.

He spotted me under the table and instantly grew angry. He called me out from my hiding place and raised his voice to ask, "did you perform *negel vasser* this morning?" He wanted to know if I washed my hands and said my prayers. These acts signified preparing for a day of serving God. They were so deeply ingrained as a part of my daily ritual, I didn't even think about doing them. And yet, today, I had skipped them. *How had he known? And why hadn't I washed my hands anyway?* I always washed my hands. I always said the prayer.

But this morning, I had done neither. And so, of course, I told him. He hit me. I bit my lip to hold back the tears. It wasn't the pain of the not-so-hard smack that stuck with me, it was the agony of the humiliation. I had no experience in hiding sins as my siblings did. They sinned all the time, little sins—stealing an extra cookie, skipping a mandatory prayer. They knew how to get away with it.

At the time, I had a secret belief that my father was the Messiah. Yes, the actual Messiah, come to fly us and all our people on his back to Israel. When we arrived, our sins would be written on our foreheads, for all to see. Nothing could be hidden. Not from my father. Not from God.

My sister Marilyn's forehead would read, I SPIT MY VEGETABLES INTO MY NAPKIN AND DO NOT SWALLOW THEM.

Syrle's would say, I SNEAKED TV AT THE COHEN'S.

Candice's would say, I WAS MEAN TO MARILYN.

And mine would be blank.

Until today.

Each night, after going to bed at 10:30, my father would rouse himself at midnight, go down to the dining room and take the heavy book of the Talmud, among other weighty volumes and study until 2:00 a.m. Then go back to sleep and wake at 6:00 a.m. to get ready for the synagogue. In between, he worked exceedingly hard to support our family.

Why wouldn't he be the Messiah? Why *not* him? He earned it because of his devotion to the Torah. Also, we were

direct descendants of King David, and it was written that the
Messiah would be a direct descendent of that king.

I didn't want to let on that I knew. It was our secret—God's
and mine.

For us, everything was about God. Every truth was in the
Talmud. Every movement was dictated by law. There is a song
we used to sing in my childhood where every verse ends with
"Because the Torah tells us so."

I fully believed that Moses climbed up a mountain to
Heaven in order to talk to God. I was sure that the Torah,
written before God created man, but mainly about a particular
group of humans, was dictated to Moses and delivered to his
people upon descending from their mountaintop meeting.

My mother's German strictness was as unyielding as my father's
religious demands. Combined, they created a household of
never-ending rules. We undertook constant, regimented praying
because of Talmudic laws. We kept constant, regimented
bedtimes, mealtimes, and risings because Mother insisted that
this was the only correct way to live. My mother was loving, yet
intransigent. She instilled in us the value of self-control. Good
manners and proper behavior were a large part of her value
system, and the lessons my mother taught us came in handy
later in life.

For Sabbath dinners, we sat up straight and ate with
flawless manners—a cloth napkin always on each one of our
laps. Regardless of our age, we were not allowed to touch our
faces, talk with food in our mouths, chew with our mouths
open, giggle, get up, or reach over other people. Chewing

raw carrots was forbidden at the Sabbath table because my father thought it made too much noise. If we were having an everyday supper in the kitchen, my father was not there, so it was okay.

My father forbade silliness, loudness, and uncouth behavior. He spent every second of his free time studying the Talmud, except for Saturday, the day of rest. For Morton, if God had given Moses an Eleventh Commandment, it would have read: *Thou Shalt Not Waste Time.* Above the kitchen sink, my father had hung up a sign, *Time is a terrible thing to waste.* Levity, small talk, and leisure time with his family—were all gratuitous.

We existed on Earth to serve God. Things such as laughter were signs that we weren't studying or working. If we were laughing, we weren't pleasing God. My mother permitted laughing but never crying.

When my little brother Mordechai turned five, he got his first *siddur* (prayer book).

His eyes lit up. He was delighted and overjoyed. We all went into the living room and gathered around the card table with cookies and a fresh-baked cake.

My father said, "You're a big boy now and you're going to learn the *Alef bais* (Hebrew alphabet) so that you can read from your very own '*siddur*'. It will help you to become a *Talmid Chacham* (Torah scholar). And when you do, *Hashem* (God) will reward you from heaven."

My father handed him the *siddur*, wrapped in a ribbon.

Mordechai tore off the wrapping paper and held the book in the air. "A *siddur* for me!"

Since he had already been taught the first letter, my father said, "Find an *Alef* (Hebrew letter 'A')." Mordechai proudly pointed to one on the first page.

At that moment, two nickels fell from above onto the card table.

"This is from God!" my father proclaimed. "This is what God gives you when you study Torah. You're going to have a lot of money the more you study."

Earlier that day, I had seen my father balance those nickels on the chandelier; and now I had seen him knock them down to my gullible brother's amazement. "A miracle!" he cried.

I had been too young to formulate my unease about this into anything more than a sick feeling in the pit of my stomach that I quickly pushed away and replaced with the joy that my little brother would be a *Talmid Chacham*.

My father was creating a dissonance between what he said and what I knew to be true and that forced me to either stop thinking or endure a rift with my family and religion.

I stopped thinking. So many things did not make sense. So many things were unexplainable. To myself, I said, "When I become an adult, I'll understand. When I get to heaven, God will explain it all. There are reasons, I just don't understand them, but they must be right because God says so. That's why we go to heaven in the first place. Life on Earth is not important." I attempted to push the frightening inconsistencies away. None of us could comprehend the universe, so why did my mind insist on things making sense?

But as much as I tried, it was impossible to *never* think, especially at night. I imagined that I was the only one in the world who thought so deeply, and it frightened me. Every night at bedtime, we had to say our prayers, and those words triggered my fears.

Who created God? What was before the universe was created? What is our purpose? Around and around, my mind spun, with no hope of answers except to wait for morning when I could bury my thoughts in ritual, or wait for the end of days when it would all be revealed.

The coins from the sky had been prophetic. After graduation, my dear little brother did become a *Talmid Chacham*. Mordechai moved to Israel to join the burgeoning Slonim community. *Maybe the nickel did fall from the sky.*

CHAPTER 5

MOTHER ALWAYS MADE A CAKE. SHE DISHED A FAIR serving to each one of the children and left one piece of cake on the platter. She placed the single piece at the center of the table.

She did this purposely, to teach us self-control. We had to sit and look at that piece of cake, our mouths watering, wishing we could have it. We had to learn not to eat the last piece of anything. When dinner was over, Mother would freeze the cake piece, and my sister Marilyn would later sneak a slice from the freezer. How she could think that my mother didn't know was beyond me. She wondered why she was always the one punished.

I was completely unable to experience any pleasure in disobedience. Unlike my friends, I never ate potato chips, French fries, candy, or any junk food. Once a year, my mother gave us a treat in our lunch bag—two chocolate squares. I was so embarrassed to let my friends see these two squares when they could enjoy their whole chocolate bar, while I lost my taste for it because of my fear of them noticing my tiny squares. We had hot dogs once a year and pasta four times a year for dinner. Ice cream was only on holidays and not more than a modest portion. Mother wanted us to be healthy. Our snacks between meals were fruits and vegetables.

Our curfew was 7:00 PM sharp, regardless of the season.

In the summer, all the other neighborhood children played outside until dark. I felt a pang of injustice. It was not so much the humiliation of having to abandon the team that got to me, but the subsequent dull hours. I would peer out my bedroom window, looking over the baseball field, watching and listening to the others laugh, swing, run, and win championships as twilight took over the night sky. It was hardest when I heard the jingles of the Good Humor truck. I had to watch the neighborhood kids line up and get their ice cream treats every night, my mouth watering, feeling sorry for myself. It's not kosher enough for us, anyhow, I said to myself wondering why it wasn't. It was just ice cream.

All I could think of was becoming an adult so I could be free and do what I pleased. *I can accept my life as it is because I am a child but, I will grow up and I will be free, and my life will change.*

I was independent. I disliked being a child and had an intense craving to grow up, be free, and live my own life.

I decided to test my independence. I hid in the broom closet. The entire family came looking for me. My mother was frantic. I heard the commotion and the consternation, but I remained in the closet with the door closed. I do not know how long I stayed there.

I remember feeling amazed that something I had done could create such a stir. Hiding was a small maneuver through which I could take control. I felt powerful.

Eventually, I stepped out of the broom closet. I saw fear mixed with relief on my mother's face, and I had a fierce feeling of strength. In some way, my act of disappearing years later was a re-enactment of this moment, a way to prove I existed in a world where I seemed not to matter at all.

I had unusually philosophical thoughts for a child. I would look at my hands, marvel at my fingers, and think about our physical being versus our mind. *Is there a separation between the two? How was the universe created? How will the world end? Moreover, where did God fit in? Why were we created in the first place? Why does God need people at all? Why would there be a God who created people—created right and wrong, good and evil—just to be born and die (knowing everything that was going to happen anyhow) for the purpose of serving him? Did he possess the human desire for power and need for love?*

Why...why...why...

Those thoughts were daunting and none of the adults had the answers. At the time, I tried to bury my thoughts. Eventually, they always bubbled back up. Years after leaving religion behind, I learned that the so-called gurus of all religions had the same answer: "God works in mysterious ways," or "It will all be clear in paradise, the real world in heaven."

Despite all of my unanswered questions, I had a benevolent view of existence. I wanted to do something great; be a heroine. I loved what life "should and could" bring. Of all the fastidiously groomed faces in our family photos, only mine showed a smile.

My brainwashing, like my parents before them, and my grandparents before them, had begun at birth. I was *tabula rasa*—a blank slate. The rituals began on my first day, carried out by my parents. The very first time my mother fed me, she said the milk blessing for me: *Blessed thou, Lord, the God of the Universe, that all was made by God.*

She made these food blessings over every morsel I ate until I was old enough to talk. Consequently, by the time I did talk, I uttered these blessings without thought. It affected me subconsciously and influenced every action and feeling. This effect only increased over my lifetime. By the time I began to think for myself, I was already too far gone to do anything about it. Yes, I had questions about the nature of my existence. Yes, neither my reading of the Talmud nor the words of my father, with all his Talmudic learning, sufficiently answered those questions. But none of this ever for a single moment cast the slightest doubt on my belief in the nature or existence of God. I only ever questioned people's abilities to explain on God's behalf. The core of my belief was untouchable.

CHAPTER 6

WHILE I LIVED FOR THE NEXT WORLD, MY CHILDHOOD wasn't unhappy. On wintery Friday nights, my sisters and I would walk home from synagogue in the freezing cold with my father, trying to keep our hands warm. Girls generally did not attend the Friday service, but we enjoyed it, so we would often go.

"Marilyn! Don't push."

"It's my turn to hold Daddy's hand."

"Daddy, Marilyn held your hand on the way there!"

Our father had the greatest hands in the world as far as we were concerned. To hold them was warm and safe and wonderful.

"Stop fighting and I'll tell you a story," he would say, and we'd all fall silent and into step with each other. He was an excellent storyteller. "Have I told you the one about the rabbi who was put in an incinerator and didn't burn?"

"You told us that one last week."

"How about the rabbi and the lion?"

"Tell us that one!" We listened, rapt.

These stories, my father would assure us, were true. They were in the Talmud. They were not metaphors or symbolic, but the literal truth of real events that had happened. "The Rabbi danced in the fire…The lion licked his hand…they were in awe and the fear of God who came to him and he bowed to the Rabbi…"

We hung on every word, walking home in the dark, holding his hand, sure that the world was a dangerous and difficult place, but that we were the chosen ones, the ones who when set upon by vicious lions, would emerge with licked hands and a new, regal pet ready to obey our every command, all by the grace of God.

But my father couldn't hold our hands forever. He understood we were growing up, going out into the world on our own. My older sisters, especially, were quickly assimilating into the larger world as they matured.

When their children reached school age, Morton and Sheila Steinberg sent them to the Hebrew Institute of Long Island, the local Modern Orthodox Day School.

The Modern Orthodox were less strict than we were: they had no balcony for women in the synagogue, just a separate section on the floor; the men wore *yarmulkes* but might take them off at the beach with no fear of creating a scandal. HILI was an excellent co-ed school, focused on carrying on traditional culture, but in a somewhat Americanized way.

This was all fine and good with my parents until the specter of interaction between boys and girls arose. By the time Candice approached 8th grade, the school had started having co-ed dances for the 8th graders. My mother voiced her strenuous objection to the HILI administration, but nothing came of it. When she heard reports of students being boyfriends and girlfriends, this was the straw that broke the camel's back. "Boys can't touch girls!" she said, adamantly. "It's not the proper way to raise religious children."

When my sisters were born, my father had brought them to the *rebbe* for a blessing. The *rebbe* cautioned my father, "Make sure they get a proper Jewish education."

"Don't forget your Jewishness," my grandfather had warned my father years before, as he watched his son adopting secular ways. All these admonitions came back to my father as he observed my two older sisters, Candice and Syrle, about to enter their high school years.

My father enrolled Candice at the Ultra-Orthodox, all-girls Beth Jacob high school in Williamsburg, Brooklyn.

Nothing would ever be the same.

Every Friday night, we had a formal Sabbath dinner. Those nights were always magical. The Sabbath began at sundown. After it started, we were not allowed to put anything in our mouths until my father had returned from the synagogue and said all of the Sabbath blessings. Starting in the early summer, this could be as late as 9:30 before my father returned from Synagogue.

We would welcome the Sabbath into our home with song, then my father would intone the *Kiddush* blessing on the wine in a melodic tone. We would respond "Amen" and Father would drink half of the cup of wine.

He would pour an ounce into each one of the girls' Sabbath wine glasses in age order, but for my two brothers, into each one of their engraved sterling silver cups, given to them at birth. Because my younger brothers were preparing to be men who would one day recite the *Kiddush* for their own families, they had larger cups than the girls.

On Saturdays, life was wonderful and the mood in our home was calm and happy.

The family walked to the synagogue dressed in our formal clothes for *Shabbos*. I loved everything about the Sabbath, including wearing my Sabbath best (a new hat and coat, new gloves, and patent leather shoes with white frilly socks, every season).

I so admired my Mother, who was modest, yet stylish. I was proud of her refinement and how she walked with grace. My mother was held in high esteem in the community and respected for her finesse and intelligence. Many were in awe of her independence and very mistakenly thought that she wore the pants in the family. There was nothing further from the truth.

At this time, in my early childhood, we dressed and looked like Americans. I was proud to be an American. If anyone asked me, "What are you?" my first answer would be, "I'm an American!" My religion was private, between myself and my God. It was not something to be announced or flaunted. We practiced our Orthodoxy with a true desire to be pious. We were Orthodox in word and deed, as well as in the spiritual sense. We kept a strictly kosher home. We read the Torah on the Sabbath. We studied and obeyed the *Talmud*. Though we were not clad in European garb like the Hasidic Jews who were growing in number around us, we observed religious law more strictly. The men with beards and *pe'us* (long side curls at the ear) and the women in their wigs, long skirts, and seamed stockings had nothing on us.

My father went to the synagogue with my two brothers an hour earlier, to ensure that they were present for the start of services. Men had to be on time. My brothers sat next to my father and didn't budge, unlike most of the children who were too restless and so would play in the auditorium. In an Orthodox synagogue, men sat in the sanctuary downstairs and women sat in the balcony upstairs. This was to prevent men from being distracted. Men were supposed to have complete concentration without looking at or thinking of women when they prayed.

My sisters and I were the only girls who sat upstairs during services. Unlike the other girls who were downstairs playing or sitting with their friends, we were carefully watched over by my mother who made sure that we concentrated on the service. We followed every word of the Torah reading by the *Baal Koreh* (the Torah reader), paying careful attention to its meaning. Since we spoke Hebrew fluently, this was not a problem. I could follow along and still admire the women around me in their beautiful hats and Sabbath clothes. We prayed and chanted:

> *"Listen, Israel, God is our God, God is one. And you shall love your God, with all of your heart, with all of your soul, and with all of your possessions. And it will be that these words which I command you today shall be upon your hearts, and you shall teach them to your sons...."*

The words all seemed to say the same thing with different adjectives, like a thesaurus. The commands and prayers were repeated over and over and quickly became rote.

> *"God is good, God is great, God is omnipotent, God is loving, God is invincible, God is Supreme, God is all-powerful, God is unlimited, O Lord, the God of Israel, there is no God like thee. We thank him for our daily bread."*

I mused, *well, we wouldn't be here if there wasn't any food. And if we weren't here, who would God have to worship him? He'd be out of luck.*

I just really wanted to know how we fit together with God. I genuinely wanted to understand. Unfortunately, this kind of questioning was frowned upon. I knew better than to say my thoughts out loud.

After services, we had the previous night's leftovers for lunch. Friday night's rituals were repeated before we could start our meal. The conversation was never frivolous. My father mesmerized us with bible stories as we ate. Table talk was dogmatic, but always thought-provoking. We were convinced that our father knew everything.

At those meals, I saw the love that my mother had for my father. When my father complimented my mother's cooking after tasting the first bite, she beamed. She looked into my father's eyes. They stared at each other and her smile reached my father at the other end of the table. She smiled ever so lovingly. That's what made her happy. Watching them gave me purpose and promised me a worthwhile future, a joyful married life to come.

And her happiness made me happy, too. Not only for my parents but because no matter how thoughts nagged at me, I knew that one day, I would be like them—happy.

A passing stranger peering into our dining room windows might think that our lives were perfect. He might think that we had it all.

And perhaps the rest of my family did.

But the divide between what I saw and thought, and what we believed, was growing. Our lives were full of beauty and tradition. I loved God and wanted him to love me.

Of course, life was far more complicated.

CHAPTER 7

S OON AFTER OUR FAMILY ARRIVED IN LONG ISLAND, another Orthodox family, the Cohens, moved in across the road. They also had six children. In other words, we had a *minyan*—the number of people required for a truly excellent game of pick-up baseball.

I was an energetic tomboy. In school, I was the captain of every sports team. The field was the only place I felt true freedom and joy. I cherished it. God was everything to me, of course, but sports were a close second. I lived every day for a ball in my hand. If I couldn't get a game together, I would play roof ball. This entailed whaling a pinky ball at the garage roof, then diving after it as it sprung off at unexpected angles. It was heaven on earth! I slept with my pinky ball. If I had had a baseball glove, I would have slept with that, too. But we had to borrow all our gear from the Cohens. Both of my brothers had a baseball and bat of their own, but my mother would never even consider buying anything as frivolous as sports equipment for girls.

By the time I was eleven, our games were still going strong even though Candice and Syrle no longer played. Their new, Ultra-Orthodox school was in Brooklyn, an hour away. They were spending time with their new school friends, who firmly believed that girls did girl things and boys did boy things, which included baseball. To fit in with their new group and because of the time their commute took, they dropped out of the Sunday games. Mordechai had joined the roster and was proving worthy of the Steinberg name.

One afternoon, we were playing the crucial last game of a seven-game World Series. The winner of this game would be Champion of the World and have perpetual bragging rights—at least until next week's World Series. I was sure we were going to win. We had to win. It felt as if my life depended on it.

Our mother rang a bell to call us back into the house.

My stomach clenched in anger and dismay, but there was nothing to be done. Mother was a force of nature. We knew for whom the bell tolled.

"No! One more pitch!" Joey Cohen begged.

But the Steinbergs had already abandoned their borrowed gloves and bats and were halfway home at a full run.

When we got to the porch my mother said, "I only need Rita. Daddy wants to speak with her." Rita was my name at the time, the name everyone called me, my American name.

The others went back to the game, more relieved than curious. I couldn't fathom what this was all about. Why would my father want to meet with me in the middle of an ordinary Sunday? And why did it have to be now?

At that moment, I was baffled but really delighted that I was getting some special attention. With six children in the family—not much time was left over for me, especially being the fourth girl. Most children might be afraid that punishment was coming for some transgression, but I knew I never did anything wrong. I couldn't wait, nor imagine—what good thing was in store for little Rita? Why was I so special to be invited to talk to my father?

I entered the dining room, and from his seat, at the head of the table my father gave me a warm smile and I relaxed. I sat to his left across from my mother. It was strange to see my mother sit by his side, instead of at the other end of the table. It was still even stranger to be sitting next to my father—this was my brother's seat. It felt ominous, but at the same time, it was exciting. I tried to concentrate, but the smack of the bat on the ball from down the street echoed over the mostly empty table. Who had taken my at-bat? What was the score?

My father said very simply, in his usual, unadorned way, "You are no longer going to be called Rita. You are now Laya."

I nodded.

"You may go now."

And so, I did. I went back out to the game, but I felt odd as if something important had just occurred—only I had no idea what. But the Messiah had spoken. Chaya Laya had always been my Hebrew name, but no one ever called me that. Now they would.

"What did he want?" Marilyn asked.

"Pitch the ball," Joey Cohen called.

"Daddy changed my name," I reported. "What's the score?"

"To what?" Mordechai asked.

"To the game, Mo," I said, rolling my eyes.

"No, I mean, he changed your name to what?"

"Oh. To Laya. My Hebrew name. What's the score?"

"You're up, Rita," Joey said.

"Laya," Marilyn corrected.

"You're still losing three-one, whoever you are."

I took the bat and headed for home, Rita/Laya at the plate.

What had it all meant? I had no idea. All my sisters had American names. It certainly wasn't a Jewish tradition, renaming the fourth child at age eleven.

I swung and missed. Then again. And missed again.

I met David at the mound, really the sewer cover in the middle of the street, so he could give me his glove.

"Your dad's weird," David said.

But what had just happened wasn't weird to me. It was just my father. It never even occurred to me to have an opinion about my new name. My father had decided on something. What he said, went. It was like my mother's bell. We obeyed. Anyway, I was back outside, back where I could run free. I didn't care what anyone called me, just so long as I got to play shortstop.

From then on, the Jewish community called me Laya while our neighbors knew me as Rita.

My life had begun to split in two. My father's attempt to quell my spirit by changing my name was fruitless. I should have seen then that my happy days on the field were numbered. My father surely saw something in my carefree, tomboy, sports-loving spirit that bothered him.

CHAPTER 8

C ANDICE HAD RECENTLY GRADUATED FROM BETH JACOB High School, and Syrle was in her senior year. Marilyn was about to start her Beth Jacob career.

She assessed herself in the mirror. "Laya, where's the center of my knee? Here?" She touched the center of her knee, the spot dictated by law where the hem of her skirt must hit.

"That looks right."

"But are you sure? Is it lower?" She moved her finger a millimeter lower.

"I don't know. Make it longer if you're nervous."

She frowned. She didn't want to make it longer. To me, Marilyn looked perfect. She was tall, thin, and elegant. She didn't want to cover an extra millimeter of her legs if she didn't have to.

"If I put it here, then walk, does it still stay in the right place?" she asked, walking confidently across her bedroom with perfect posture.

"You're overdoing it, Mal. That's not the rule *when you walk*."

"I don't want to go to hell." *But I want to show my legs.*

"What about my sleeves?" she asked.

"You look perfect," I told her. "You'll be the most beautiful girl in school."

"This is Beth Jacob," she said. "It's more religious than HILI" - the Jewish day school I was still two years away from completing. We learned Jewish studies from 8:30 to 12:30 in Hebrew, then spent the other half of the day acquiring a secular education in English.

"I love Hili," I told Marilyn. I loved my baseball team and my volleyball team. I loved recess and science class, and I was especially proud when I received my first science award.

A shadow passed over Marilyn's face.

"What?" I asked, searching for an explanation for the abrupt change in her expression. Half glee, half foreboding.

She shrugged. "Mom and Dad are taking you out of Hili."

My stomach sank. "How do you know?"

She shrugged again, but she didn't need to answer. I already knew how she knew. She was the resident eavesdropper and was thrilled to be my informant. "Next year you're going to Beth Jacob, too. They're not going to wait until you graduate eighth grade as we did. But you're lucky because Hili is much harder than Beth Jacob."

I did not like this one bit. "I like hard. I like to study. I want to stay with my friends at Hili. And school in Brooklyn? Where Aunt Eva and Uncle Aaron live?" I knew Williamsburg, Brooklyn only as of the unhygienic neighborhood where my aunt and uncle lived with my nine cousins in a tiny row house with bars on their windows. When we went to visit, we had to walk down five steps and pass through two metal gates into their narrow, confined house. They had three bedrooms for eleven people.

"Hili is not religious enough for us anymore. We're not supposed to go to school with boys." Marilyn did a final check in the mirror. She looked perfect. Later, when she started dating, I would stand by as she rehearsed her conversations with the boys beforehand, so she could sound smart, too.

Though my sisters had loved their time there, the moment I started Beth Jacob's junior high I felt displaced.

The girls at Beth Jacob were Haredi, or Ultra-Orthodox, a fast-growing sect of Judaism that embraced every zealous, onerous law they could scrape from the Talmud, plus the countless new Rabbinical restrictions. They followed these laws to a tee and claimed their brand of Judaism as the only authentic practice. This fanaticism was spreading throughout our increasingly insular Orthodox community, infecting young and old, turning centuries of tradition into a cult. Paradoxically, this Great Leap Backward was being led by the youth.

Those in the now thriving Jewish-American communities were wracked with survivor's guilt after the Holocaust. Their European counterparts had suffered and died in the war while they sat in relative safety. They also saw how the German government had turned on the Jewish communities, even though they were completely integrated into their society. Many realized that they could not depend on their national identities and responded in one of two ways. Reform and Conservative Jews became Zionists and the Orthodox decided to get back to their European religious roots and have large families to replenish the numbers lost. There was an old joke that I didn't get at the time: *We named the baby Shlomo after his grandfather, Scott.*

Candice quickly embraced the Ultra-Orthodox ideology she found at her new school. In those early days, it seemed innocent enough. She was getting excited about her faith. For the first time in her life, she found a group of peers to share a passion with. She loved it. She was in her new comfort zone.

My father did not don a beard. He wore a yarmulke at all times. But I can remember one day when he took me to work with him, I saw him walking around the plant without a yarmulke on his head. I was shocked. I didn't say a word to him, but as soon as I came home, I ran to my mother and said, "Daddy didn't wear a yarmulke in the office today. How come?"

She answered me, "Sometimes in a secular environment you don't have to wear a *yarmulke* and make your religion so obvious."

My father loved our country. He loved being an American. Both of my parents appreciated the secular culture and did not feel that it interfered with their devoutness to God. And before the rise of Ultra-Orthodoxy, my parents were two of the most pious people in our community.

But it wasn't enough for Candice. Beth Jacob had offered her a new identity, community, and sense of belonging. She jumped at the chance and stopped seeing the friends from her old, less religious, school.

"Mom, give these t-shirts to someone else. I am going to need some more modest blouses. And please, get rid of these pants. I need some skirts long enough to wear to school" my sister said, as she threw her entire closet into a plastic bag.

One day, Candice came home from school and eyed me nervously.

"What?" I asked, bewildered.

"Please change into a dress," she said. "I have friends coming over and I don't want them to see you wearing pants."

I didn't understand, but I would do anything for my sister. I certainly did not want her to be embarrassed.

That was my first encounter with Ultra-Orthodoxy. Even as a little girl, though, I did not agree that pants had anything to do with religion. It seemed absurd to me.

Syrle, who admired Candice greatly, entered Beth Jacob two years later. She also revered the life of the Ultra-Orthodox. Now both my sisters were wearing stockings under their long skirts and talking of marrying *yeshiva* boys. This disturbed my mother, who disapproved of the *yeshiva* boys' lack of manners. They chewed too loudly at the table. They lacked etiquette, nonreligious discourse, and a grasp of basic grammar. She also was not fond of their overtly religious way of dressing.

But my sisters didn't see it that way. They were being transformed by Beth Jacob High School. Candice and Syrle entered that building as Jewish girls from 1960s America. They graduated resembling Eastern European women from the sixteenth century.

Candice graduated at sixteen when I was only nine. A year later, the matchmaker knocked on our door. "It's time to find Candice a good husband," she said.

Candice had decided to attend seminary to further study the finer points of Jewish womanhood while she looked for her husband, but her education was not important. She also went to a secular college but dropped out after six months. A secular education would have tainted her reputation as a proper Jewish wife. When my parents met, my mother's college education was one of the things my father had admired about her, but that had been another time, another way of thinking. We were moving backward so quickly. The recent past was a blur of confusion and contradiction. On Candice's third date, she met a *yeshiva* boy she liked. He proposed, and she happily accepted with my father's blessing.

"He wants to study Talmud," Candice assured my father.

My father wouldn't have it any other way.

He agreed with great joy to support their family for five years. Candice completed seminary and with her new husband moved to Lakewood, New Jersey, where they were among the first twenty Ultra-Orthodox families in what is now a huge Ultra-Orthodox community.

Within a year, Candice had her first baby, a boy, and with each passing year, eight more followed.

Two years later, when I was thirteen, the matchmaker was back at our door, this time for Syrle.

Syrle took to the Ultra-Orthodox crowd with as much fervor as our oldest sister. When she graduated at seventeen, the matchmaker arranged a date between her and the nephew of a famous Jewish scholar, a scion of a renowned dynasty.

"He's the catch of the century, the smartest eligible bachelor in the Ultra-Orthodox Jewish world," the matchmaker told my father.

"And he knows it," my mother lamented. He would not even date a girl unless her father had signed a contract to support his studies for at least fifteen years.

"I'll sign for twenty!" declared my delighted father. The week after Syrle was engaged, my future brother-in-law flew to Israel to decide if the Holy Land was the place where they should live their lives together. The day after he returned, they were married. Their baby boy was born nine months later,

During his trip, Syrle's new husband had studied in the strictest yeshiva in Jerusalem for three months and decided it was the holiest place he could raise a family. Eleven months after their marriage, they moved to Israel with their two-month-old baby.

"Will I ever see her again?" I asked my mother.

"Surely. If not in this world, in the next."

Wrong answer. I was miserable. "I miss her already. I miss the baby."

In fact, I missed both of my sisters. And not only because they had moved away. I missed the old Candice, who played baseball with me in the street and who didn't wear stockings and a wig. I missed the old Syrle, who climbed trees with me in the one-block forest between our home and the train station. Marilyn, who was the only one to prepare me for my first period, would marry only two years later and soon had her first baby.

Although I was overjoyed with all my nieces and nephews, I knew that my family had changed forever. Would I be next?

CHAPTER 9

I DID NOT RELATE TO MY CLASSMATES AT BETH JACOB Middle School.

Although I had an attractive home, with a large backyard in the suburbs, I secretly envied those Brooklyn girls for their short walks to school from their mysterious row houses with iron gates and black metal bars on every window. That fascinated me. I didn't realize at the time it was to keep out of danger. I was oblivious to danger. I just loved what seemed like a million kids on the street to play with and the stores you could walk to and buy kosher treats. I yearned for the camaraderie and after-school playdates these city-girls shared instead of getting back in the car for the long boring ride back to my regimented, always proper home.

It became increasingly clear that although this school was ultra-religious, and I was as devout as they came, I didn't fit in there. The place was devout in appearance, but when it came time for prayer, I was the only one genuinely engaged.

The girls were like middle school girls everywhere and gathered in cliques. But I was not that way at all. I was destined to be lonely and unhappy at Beth Jacob Middle School.

Fortunately, I had dodgeball. It was the only break in my stultified life there. Linda, my best friend from my neighborhood, and I would take on the whole grade in the narrow street in front of the school. Two against the world! We'd always win. It was remarkably cathartic to slam those balls into the other girls who knew I didn't fit in. I was vicious, but solely in the name of the game of course. In my heart, I was pure.

"If only you paid more attention to your studies like you do dodgeball, you'd be the smartest girl in my class," my eighth-grade teacher whispered to me. Disenchanted with the school, regretfully, I never took heed.

Nevertheless, I ran for Vice President of my school, and hung up the marketing material that I created on my own, on every stairwell, so each student would notice while navigating from class to class. I wanted to create change and felt certain of my convictions.

On voting day, I was confident. We all stood in the hallway, anticipating the announcement of the winner: *"Laya Steinberg—Vice President!"*

My perseverance was rewarded. I did not allow being an outsider of the class to get in my way. It was my first feeling of leadership—to move the world forward.

I made my way through the two years of junior high and went on to Beth Jacob High School. The building was an old, abandoned public school, with narrow hallways and dingy stairwells. There was no gymnasium, no room for art or music, and not even a science lab. After all, we didn't believe in evolution, so who needed science? There was no space for an athletic field (not that we played sports anyway), and not even any grass to sit in under the trees. Instead, we perched on the narrow concrete stoops, shifting our positions every time someone wanted to go in or out of the building.

By the time I reached high school, my sisters had graduated. My mother drove me to the subway station in Queens and I rode the A train to Brooklyn alone. Beth Jacob High School was in Williamsburg and the hub of the fundamentalist Jewish community. Everywhere you looked were men with long beards, little boys with side curls, and women wearing hats to cover their *sheitals* (wigs) and long skirts to cover their antiquated seamed stockings. Townspeople carried bags of various goods to and from the marketplace.

In my family, the purpose of life was to develop one's own substance, intellect, and religious devotion. Our accomplishments were what counted; material possessions were far less important. When I met others, I always focused on substance.

At Beth Jacob, the utmost importance was placed on how you looked and how well you adhered to community rules. Keeping up appearances came first. Character, integrity, and virtue came in a distant second.

I came to school one morning wearing white socks. At the door to the school, a teacher stood sentry. "Laya, are you wearing stockings?" she asked.

"Yes, I am." I knew what was coming and felt sickened.

"Just a moment." She bent down and ran her hands up my legs to check for stockings under my white bobby socks. "Okay. You may go in now."

I hurried into the building.

It was offensive being groped like that, and insulting that she didn't trust me to obey the rules. But when I complained to my mother about the shoddy treatment, she replied "It's just the rules. They have to make sure girls don't go astray and become immodest." She said it half-heartedly. It wasn't the way she was raised.

These dress codes were derived from rabbinic rulings on Jewish law. Even though the women were quick to embrace them, the rules had nothing to do with women. They were there to stop men from being distracted by their libidos. Apparently, these rabbis thought a lot about women and sexuality, considered the thoughts bad, and decided it was the woman's job to fix it. It must not have occurred to them that the rest of the country was walking around in miniskirts and tank tops and somehow getting along all right.

One does wonder, though: if the male mind is thrown so wildly off course by glimpsing a set of feminine elbows, maybe God should have entrusted the more level-headed women with the great knowledge and responsibilities.

But we were not to wonder why.

You are to whom you are born.

Take a walk down Wall Street in Manhattan, and you will see Hasidic Jews who appear no different than they might have 100 or 200 years ago. They have long beards and coats and a small strand of curly hair called the "*pe'us*." Drive to Lancaster, Pennsylvania, and you'll see the Amish dressed as they did three hundred years ago.

The truth is that the majority of people follow the path they were born into, regardless of the pervading culture. The number of people who maintain the same religion as their parents still represents the vast majority. Few people have the courage or even the desire to buck the norms of the cultures in which they are raised.

Miriam was no exception. In my senior year, she was the first of my classmates to become engaged.

"Oh, Miriam, that's wonderful," we all cried in unison.

"And the night after my wedding, I'm shaving my head."

The cries of joy turned to gasps of horror, then silence.

We looked at one another, not knowing what to say. For once, we all agreed: this was too far. We were Ultra-Orthodox, but we weren't fanatics.

"I'm Satmar," she said as if that justified this appalling ritual. "I cannot let other men be tempted." Satmar was a particularly strict sect of Hasidim. My Hasidic, Slonim dynasty, although different from the Haredi sect that most of my classmates belonged to, shared the same marriage traditions. We would cover our hair with a wig when we married, but only Satmar women would shave their heads.

"How could you?" a girl cried in disbelief.

"Women did that two hundred years ago."

"This is America."

"Your hair is so gorgeous!" I said. "Don't you want your husband to see your hair and not a bald head?" I shuddered as I imagined a lifetime of a hot, itchy wig on her shaved scalp—such unnecessary humiliation and constant discomfort. Of course, we would all be required to wear hot, heavy wigs *over* our hair from the day we married to the day we died, but at least, we rationalized, we weren't as bad off as Miriam.

Miriam shrugged. "My mother shaves her head, and I am happy to do it too. My betrothed doesn't want me to tempt other men." Those were the rules of modesty bestowed upon her, and she was proud to accept them.

But what was happening in my house was subtly different. No woman in my family had ever worn wigs. So, when Candice had become engaged years before, she approached my mother with determination.

"When can we go to downtown Brooklyn to look at some wigs? I'm going to need one for the daytime and a nicer one for *Shabbos* and the holidays. I have to be fitted and they have to be ready by my wedding date." A girl had to obtain the wig as soon as possible after her engagement. It was more important than the wedding dress. The dress was worn once, but the wig was worn every day of a married woman's life.

Mother winced but went along with it because this is what her daughter wanted. She felt these fundamentalist practices were unnecessarily burdensome. To my mother's way of thinking, they didn't represent religious devotion. The notion that these practices harken back to anything biblical or "authentically" Jewish was patently ridiculous. As the best-selling Israeli author Yuval Harari points out in his book *Sapiens:*

> *"If King David were to show up in an Ultra-Orthodox synagogue in present-day Jerusalem, he would be utterly bewildered to find people dressed in east European clothes, speaking, in a German dialect (Yiddish) and having endless arguments about the meaning of a Babylonian text (the Talmud). There were neither volumes of Talmud nor even Torah scrolls in ancient Judaea."*

Absurd as these dress codes were, to flout them was to risk being ostracized or even excommunicated. By the time Syrle wed her yeshiva boy and put on her wig, my mother's disdain was more muted. She was getting used to it. When Marilyn, her third daughter, married and covered her beautiful hair, my mother said, "I guess it's time for me to start wearing a wig, too."

And for their sake, she did. She had become what she spurned. No one wants to be different. No one wants to be alone. The pull of community is powerful, and my mother, one of the strongest women I know, gave in without a fight. It disturbed me deeply. My mother was a wonderful, pious, modest woman. It was impractical for her to wear an uncomfortable wig every day. Besides, it was about men. Part of forming a community is making rules that must be followed at the cost of being cast out.

Miriam knew this. My mother knew this. Even I knew this. Although I was modest by my own standards, when the time came I would follow the same dress code and wear a wig, too.

Years later, my sister told my eighty-three-year-old maternal grandmother that if she didn't put on a wig, she would not go to heaven. Her husband had always been vehemently opposed to women wearing wigs. In his opinion, the wig was nonsense. But my grandmother, widowed and vulnerable, put on the wig. It broke my heart.

My father, who had grown up in a much more religious community until he was eleven and came to America, was happy to see his children return to his roots. It was nostalgic. His children would be raised in an environment more similar to his own rearing than he could have imagined. Perhaps because of his disappointments and the vicissitudes of life, he felt he had made a mistake in Americanizing himself and his family.

My father was a conflicted man. He lacked certainty. He loved America and at the same time, he was laden with guilt, or perhaps fear. Perhaps he was so supportive of my family's new-old ways because he felt they exonerated his sin of secularizing. He was delighted that those around him dressed as they did, although he was still an American and a businessman and couldn't bring himself to wear the black suits and fur hats of his sons-in-law. Soon, this would change. When that time came, I knew he was no longer an American like me.

To me, it all felt like defeat. Everything inside me felt blocked by religion. The leaders of our community told us what was good and what was right. They told us what to think and what to do. And we did it, even if it didn't make sense.

It was on dark wintery Friday nights after my three sisters had married and moved away, when I would sit in the living room with my mother, waiting for my father to come home from synagogue. As I waited, my thoughts would wander. I could not stop my mind from thinking.

My anxiety grew as the clock on the wall tick-tick-ticked the hours, the days, the months. There was a vast void where substantive answers should be. Something was not adding up.

I turned to my mother and asked, *"When did it all start? Why did God need to create us? What happens when everybody is dead? No more world? Is everything heaven? Why then have the world?"* My mother had no idea why I would ask questions like these, nor could she understand them.

This endless path of questions snowballed until I finally worked myself into an existential crisis. Later on, that night, I had grown so disturbed that I told my mother I couldn't fall asleep.

"Are you letting your thoughts go everywhere again?"

"Why have a world? It doesn't make sense!"

"Let's speak to your father."

My father had an answer. "Take her to a doctor," he told my mother. "This isn't normal for a girl to be so deep in her thoughts."

The doctor gave me medicine to "relax" my mind.

I tried it once. It didn't help.

My parents didn't understand my state of mind and it wasn't their fault. My father had been indoctrinated since infancy to believe that girls had no business thinking about anything but babies and husbands. His belief was "You live, and you die, and that's it." He had no answers, and it seemed as if he didn't care for any. Anything he didn't understand would be revealed to him in Heaven by God himself.

My father was indeed a learned man. Yet somewhere along the way, all of that knowledge blinded him from seeing his daughter's curiosity as anything important. His beliefs forced him to surrender his own philosophical autonomy.

I was too frightened to confess my state of mind to anyone at school or outside my family. The possibility didn't even occur to me. I was so good at being good that no one at my school and none of my friends ever knew how terrified I often was. I desperately needed companionship, someone to explain things to me.

CHAPTER 10

THE SUMMER BREEZE HAD BLOWN IN FROM HEAVEN, breaking the chains of compulsory education. I had finally graduated from Beth Jacob High School.

I was ready for the voyage that would become the rest of my life. A week after graduation I would leave to be a counselor at Camp Greenberg, a world of Orthodox Jewish culture and companionship. Then, after a glorious summer of sun and friendship, I would come home, go to Seminary, marry a yeshiva boy, have as many children as I could, and be a good Jewish wife. It all seemed as if it were ordained by God.

Camp Greenberg was an all-girls Jewish community, just like school, but at camp, I was able to be a tomboy in a way that was forbidden at Beth Jacob. The camp had volleyball courts, baseball fields, an obstacle course, arts and crafts, swimming pools, and a large, beautiful lake. We played games and sports around the clock, went on hikes, performed in plays, and had all-girl dances.

During those summers, I found camaraderie with the other girls that I never found in school. We would pick blackberries on the shores of a beautiful lake, spit out the sour ones, and wrangle over the sweet ones. Summer camp was the only time I truly felt free as a teenager. Our structured days felt relatively loose to me. I controlled my own destiny. During my summer as a counselor, I discovered an identity that fit me and found true friendship. I loved it and loved myself in it.

It was six days before the first day of camp.

"Any student or graduate of Beth Jacob who attends or is employed by Camp Greenberg shall be barred from attending The Beth Jacob Seminary School program." The seminary was a two-year program designed to replace college for Ultra-Orthodox women. A girl could continue her education there while she looked for a husband without losing status.

My mother picked up the letter, read it, then passed it on to my father.

"It says barred," my mother said as she blanched at the realization. "What if they bar Laya from...?"

"Nonsense," my father said, as he tossed the edict from the rabbis aside.

"Someone at Camp Greenberg offended someone at Beth Jacob." He muttered under his breath.

"They won't bar my daughter from the seminary over a squabble between the Rabbis. It's just politics. The camp being sacrilegious—absurd. These kinds of disagreements happen. They'll work it out by the fall. Of course, you'll go to the seminary," he assured me.

I read the letter with its stern, absolute decree, but I was also unafraid, sure I would still go to the Beth Jacob Seminary in the fall if my father said so.

The discussion about camp was over.

I was relieved and grateful that my father would let me go to summer camp. I wasn't the slightest bit nervous. After all, my father was a powerful man. And he was never wrong. In the back of my mind, he was still the Messiah.

Being a counselor was every bit the joy I expected. I loved the playful nine-year-old children in my bunk, and the feeling was mutual.

I loved children. I always had. From the tiniest babies to the most awkward pre-teens. At night, I put my girls to bed, then went to find the other counselors. After a few nights of sitting around the camp, we were bored.

"Let's hitchhike into town," I said.

"Laya! We can't!"

"Why not? We'll split up in pairs and hitch rides. It will be fun!"

It worked. We had a ball, doing what we wanted. It was my first taste of real independence—and leadership. My first taste of what it would mean to be an adult.

On visiting day, my parents came to see me.

"Laya, look at you!" my mother gushed. "The country air is doing you wonders! You're so tan! And look at those highlights in your hair."

My father wasn't as pleased. My glowing skin and radiant health proved that something out of his control was causing me joy.

A week later, my mother telephoned on behalf of my father. "Your father said that you must inform the head counselor that you're leaving. It's time for you to come home and work for him."

"Mom, do I really have to come home? I love it here."

My mother knew it was unfair. But she only sighed and said, "It's what your father wants."

Any normal teenager would have said, *but why would Dad take away the very thing that means the most to me? I'm so happy here!* But I knew the deal: I had to obey my father under all circumstances until the day this responsibility was passed on to my husband. Which, come to think of it, probably encouraged my sisters to wed so young.

I said, "Okay," and hung up the phone.

The community gossip used to whisper: *Sheila wears the pants in the family.* They saw my mother as a strong woman with a take-charge personality, a leader in school events, and assumed that she set the rules. Only inside the family did we know the truth. My mother, like the rest of us, had no say at all.

I decided to try Candice. Out of all six children, Candice was the only one who was close to my father. She engaged *in real* conversations with him, which no one else had. And, since Candice had set the stage for all of us to gravitate toward Ultra-Orthodoxy, she had garnered special regard from my father for her devoutness.

"Candice," I begged, "I don't want to leave camp. Would you please call Dad and convince him to let me stay?"

Candice's efforts were valiant, but my father had decided and nothing would alter his decision. At the end of the week, I left. I wasn't angry or fussy. I wasn't rebellious or vengeful. I was, as always, resigned. I existed to please my parents and God. I moved on.

Years later, I learned the story of when my father was a young man and his own father demanded that he leave the yeshiva in Europe to return to New York to help run the family business. He was a brilliant student and the leaders of the school thought he was destined to be the next *Rebbe*. Still, when my grandfather called him, he came right home. By making me obey his commands in the same way, my father may have felt that he was making me a better person.

Perhaps he attributed the man he was today to the boy who followed the path that was laid out for him.

Just like in *The Godfather*, culture, tradition, and family ruled. I, like Michael Corleone, might stray, but eventually, I'd be pulled back in. We not only had no choice, but we both turned out to be naturals in the family business.

I finished the summer working for my father at his textile business. It didn't provide the fresh air and excitement that was found at Camp Greenberg, but it was rewarding in other ways. Although my tasks may have seemed mundane from an outsider's perspective: delivering samples and arranging for shipping; placing calls and answering phones, I pursued these tasks like I was born to do them. My world has always been one of perpetually delayed gratification. I defined myself by my ability to work toward the reward promised to me in the afterlife. In business, however, I worked to produce something that day, that hour even! The rewards were immediate. As soon as I crossed the threshold into the office, I came ALIVE!

A few weeks after working for my father I took textile samples to a customer and convinced them to buy from us. It was exciting! I felt so comfortable. *It's so easy to be a salesperson, I thought to myself. Is business this easy? What's the big deal?*

It seemed to be so easy to become rich and so much more fun than sitting in the office answering phones and taking orders. I'd rather be free and be the best salesman. Build a business—that's what I'll do! When I returned to the office, I couldn't understand why my father had an ecstatic grin on his face.

"Do you know how proud I am?" My father was surprised and delighted.

"You actually sold the customer on the samples. They're sending us a purchase order for 2,000 yards. They were impressed with your youth and business abilities. Do you understand what a talent that is?"

It was an exhilarating learning experience, a chance to do something meaningful and do it well.

A few months into the job, my father sent me to the office of a trucking company one block away. He was interested in hiring them to deliver rolls of textiles to Chicago. I walked down the long avenue block. I opened the door to a macho room of scruffy men, with bulging muscles. A female secretary sat quietly at the front desk with calendar pictures of naked women all over the walls. I had never seen anything like this before. I was filled with embarrassment, shock, and anger that such behavior was allowed in an office—*How can they be allowed to hang up photos of naked women in an open office?*

Embarrassed, with my head swimming, yet firm and with resolve, I asked the manager if they shipped to Chicago.

"Yes, we do," he answered without looking up.

I then confidently strode back into my father's office.

"Dad, they do ship to Chicago."

He looked up from his papers. "How many rolls will they take?"

"I...don't know," I said. I slunk back through the doorway and headed back to the trucking company. A while later, I came back into his office, this time more sheepish.

"They'll take a hundred rolls."

He looked up from his papers. "Good. What's the price?"

Oh no. "I, uh. I don't know."

"Do they pick up on Mondays and Wednesdays? How many days does it take to get there? Are they insured? For how much?"

My face was flushed with embarrassment. "Sorry. I'll be back." I turned to leave, ashamed.

"Laya," my father said before I reached the door. I turned around, ready for the verbal lashing I had seen him dish my siblings and his employees, but that I had always avoided.

"The difference between a boss and an employee is that an employee seeks answers to the questions that will fulfill his job requirements. But a boss thinks ahead and seeks to answer every question that will get the job done. Think like a boss." He smiled as he said the last words.

I was astounded and enlightened. He had given me advice in the calm voice he used when discussing business with peers. I immediately understood the difference between the two types of people: leaders create their lives using a broader vision, they are the ones who make things happen, gathering information and laying the groundwork to achieve a larger goal.

Followers stumble through life with tunnel vision, completing each task for the sake of fulfilling their assigned duties. Some wonder why things happen, others simply watch things happen, but I wanted to be like my father and *make things happen*. It was an invaluable lesson that I absorbed and have applied throughout my life. The more time we spent at work together, the more I began to understand my father and marvel at his business acumen.

On the train to work one morning he said, "I regret firing Thomas."

I was surprised. Thomas had been our operations manager until my father had dismissed him two weeks earlier in a fit of rage after witnessing what he felt was an act of incompetence. He was a difficult and explosive boss, constantly reprimanding everyone (except me).

"I underestimated how much work he was doing. I thought I could do it myself. It's a mistake to think that you can run the whole show on your own. Even the greatest thinkers are only as good as their team." He went back to his newspaper as if he hadn't just shaken my entire world.

However, this was not closeness between father and daughter, but simply a learning experience between employer and employee. The estrangement between us wasn't gone, but I was on my way to becoming an entrepreneur.

The summer ended. I headed to Beth Jacob Seminary to register for fall classes. The secretary at the registrar's office took one look at my records and raised an eyebrow.

"Are you Laya Steinberg?"

"Yes, I am."

"Your records show that you worked at Camp Greenberg this summer. Weren't you aware that this camp was forbidden to Beth Jacob students?"

I just stared at her, confused.

"It appears that you are barred from attending our seminary,"

I didn't protest. I just walked out, stunned. Those few weeks in tainted territory negated a life of perfect behavior. I would no longer get an education that was strictly biblical and traditionally Jewish. There was nothing to be done because this was the only seminary for girls in New York City.

One of the strangest things you see when you look back on life is how much of it was dictated by random events beyond your control. Our dreams are often diverted by distant decisions that have nothing to do with us.

Until that moment I knew with every fiber of my being that I would graduate high school, go to seminary, and become a wife, mother, and Hebrew teacher. In an instant, those doors were violently shut, severing me from the woman I was destined to become.

As my father had predicted, Camp Greenberg became acceptable again the following year.

But, of course, the camp had never been the issue. Internal political squabbles had radically changed my future.

Not going to seminary was a disaster of, well, biblical proportions. It was a huge step down in our community to not have a Seminary education. I had dropped in status and was forced to walk a path of lesser sanctity: the teaching program at Yeshiva University, a highly selective private university that provided secular as well as Jewish education.

How low was it? It was open to non-Jews.

Perhaps because he himself had attended Yeshiva University, my father did not put up a fight.

He would live to regret this.

CHAPTER 11

ALL THE STUDENTS SEEMED RUSHED AND EXCITED AT Yeshiva University. They looked free.

I strode down Lexington Avenue to Yeshiva University's Campus to attend the Hebrew college of Teachers Institute for Women with my head held high. Excitement arose within me. *This will be a new experience,* I thought. *I wonder what it will be like to go to college—a home of learning, for mostly secular girls only.* Though slightly detoured, the plan for my life was still on schedule. My first day was greeted with a mixture of conflicting thoughts. *I think I'm gonna like it here. But...I'm not supposed to like it here?* Still, I felt for the first time that I belonged at school, unlike the six years of discomfort at Beth Jacob. These were my kind of young girls, friendly without judging your mode of dress. *I was free.*

I delivered my first speech in Hebrew in front of our class, starting with: *Eretz Yisroel b'lee Torah, he k'goof b'lee neshama.* This translates in English to "The Land of Israel without the Torah, is likened to a body without a soul." The speech went on to express my passionate belief that, although the Jews finally had the safety net of their own country, it had become a secular country comprised of Zionists. It lacked the essence of biblical teachings, and its unholiness pained me. How could we have our Holy Land when the people there didn't respect the sanctity of the Five Books of Moses? My classmates were captivated by my fervor.

Nothing I encountered in this great center of learning shook my belief in the supreme truth of the literal word of God. When I read about evolution, I thought it was utter nonsense. I reacted to it the way most people respond when they learn about Creationism: this is just religious brainwashing. It's bad science. People only invented it because they like to tell themselves stories that confirm what they already believe. We already knew all the facts we needed because, as we sang, "The Torah tells us so!"

Nineteen-year-old boys being drafted and flown off to Vietnam. Dr. Martin Luther King Jr. and Robert Kennedy were assassinated. Urban neighborhoods erupting in fire and smoke. Protestors shouting at the gates of the White House. Women asserting their right to be heard and treated as equals. The events of the late 60s boomed and echoed throughout the world, and although Yeshiva University accepted secular students, the Jewish environment insulated me from these turbulent times. No one burned a draft card or a bra on campus. Secular students aside, we were still living for the next world.

My Jewish values were firmly rooted in me, and although I wasn't hitchhiking to a music festival or handing flowers out in Central Park, I was starting to experience the world outside of Ultra-Orthodoxy. I began attending the *Barbizon School of Modeling* two evenings a week at my mother's encouragement. Not that I *wanted* to be a model, that was out of the question. I was there to be educated on how to be a good conversationalist, how to dress with style, apply makeup elegantly, and dine with flawless manners. We were taught how to stand while waiting for someone, how to walk down the stairway elegantly, as well as how to walk a runway. The lessons on good etiquette and graceful behavior Barbizon provided gave me a sense of decorum in my day-to-day living.

What surprised me the most was the importance and the quality placed on the girls at this school. They taught us the importance of being smart, unusually good conversationalists; to be knowledgeable of politics, and to be able to form our opinions intellectually. "If you don't have the patience or time to read the newspaper," they would say, "cut out *one* single article, paste it in the bathtub, and read it while you're bathing. You must be well-informed of the world." We weren't just pretty or beautiful women, we were smart women, who could hold our own and were cognizant of the world we lived in.

I was brought up to think what was most important in a woman was that she be beautiful and have a high pedigree. I never attributed intellectual ability or knowledge as being sought-after traits for a girl. Being smart was a boy's game. After all, our reward in heaven was based on what our husbands had accomplished on earth, not our own worthiness.

These teachings vastly changed the value I attributed to myself and other women. Maybe beauty wasn't as necessary as I had thought it to be and definitely didn't speak to the multitude of core values of a person.

Toward the end of the semester, I received a call from the modeling school director. She had chosen me to represent Barbizon at the upcoming modeling school exposition at the New York Coliseum. This was a coveted opportunity. The expo was where young "unknowns" could be discovered by major modeling agencies and finally get their big break.

But I wasn't waiting for my big break.

"Thank you," I replied, quite surprised. "I'm sorry, but I must turn this down. My religious upbringing would not allow this."

"How could you turn this down?" the director asked, dumbfounded. "This has *never* happened to us before. Are you sure you understand what I'm saying? Do you realize what an honor this is?"

Bewildered, she said goodbye.

Ideologically and religiously, I was as committed a believer as I had ever been and in complete alignment with my family. In everyday living, though, my life started looking a lot less like my sisters' lives.

At night, I was studying to become a Hebrew School teacher at Yeshiva University and taking more education and social justice courses at Hunter College. This left my days free so I could work for my father.

Six months later I found myself wanting more.

"What are you saying, Laya?" my father asked. "That I should pay you?"

"Of course not," I said. *Why would a person be paid for working for their father, who fed them, clothed them, and paid for everything they needed or had? I never dreamed of taking a paycheck from my father.* "It's just that I want to find a job on my own."

"A Jewish American Princess does not go out and work for just anyone," my father said. "A girl from a family of high stature knows her role in the world. Working for her family is okay, but then she dates, gets married, and has children. Her husband works to support her. That's how it is!"

What a crazy conundrum. The obvious contradiction was that my father, at that very moment, was supporting the Talmudic studies of his two sons-in-law while his daughters worked to help ease the burden. But my sisters taught Sunday school, which was an acceptable way for a woman to spend her time. It all played into his dream of having a stable of sons who studied Talmud and dutiful, observant daughters. But at the time, the irony was lost on both of us.

I remained undeterred, and because he didn't directly forbid me, I looked for other work. I didn't care as much about the money as I cared about working for a business where I could advance on merit alone, and not rely solely on my father. So innocent and inexperienced at eighteen, I did not understand the value of money and the importance of accumulating wealth for a better life. I did not intend to stay the boss's daughter forever. Either way, we both knew that it wouldn't be long before I would be engaged and married. I placed an ad under *situations-wanted* in The New York Times, seeking a part-time office position.

It must have been clear to my father that I wanted independence, and my desire to get a real job was a sign that I was moving in the wrong direction. He was insightful enough to notice that a change was taking place in me long before I did. I had already begun to drift away.

"I found a job at a computer company," I told my parents.

"What is a computer company?" my mother asked.

My father, to my amazement, allowed me to accept the job. *Accept it!* I believe this happened because he thought it would only be temporary.

My father told my mother, "It's time we called the *matchmaker.*"

CHAPTER 12

SHIDDUCH IS AN ANCIENT MATCHMAKING TRADITION among Orthodox singles. The matchmaker, or *shadchan*, is anyone who makes those inquiries and arranges the date, from friends and relatives to professional *shadchanim (plural for Shadchan)*.

The *shidduch* system is arranged dating, not arranged marriage. Each individual has the right to accept or reject the proposal. Orthodox singles rely on the *shidduch*, a match-making tradition that dates to the time of Abraham. Instead of blindly wandering among the tribe, randomly seeking a spouse, potential partners are thoroughly vetted before they are introduced.

My father was the first in our community to use a professional *shadchan*. Today, you can hardly be a pious parent without one. The average *shadchan* will run around $2,000, but families who want to make a more highly desired match can pay over $50,000. *Highly desired* means the match has beauty, character, intelligence, and most importantly, a family with *yichus* (fine pedigree) and money.

In my generation, parents started to scout their future children-in-law when their own daughters turned seventeen. *Shadchanim* dig deep. They ask about hobbies, values, and strong and weak points. *Shadchanim* learn whether the person is serious or funny, their attitude toward money, and how clean their bedroom is. Also important is how often a person prays or *davens* and how seriously they take learning. Then parents, friends, and relatives are interrogated. They're asked more pointedly about any "deficiencies" the person might have.

To withhold this information is an unthinkable transgression. I was told about my date's flaws before we met. I knew more about him than he knew about himself.

If the father finds the *shadchan's* choice worthy, a date is set. The dates are structured as purposeful affairs. Every *shidduch* must be oriented around *tachlis,* Hebrew for "purpose." The *tachlis* of the date is to determine whether the pair is a good match for marriage and raising a family. Romance and flirting would impair a person's ability to objectively evaluate the possible mate and are discouraged. Dating can be enjoyable, but any form of entertainment would distract from the *tachlis.* Of course, any physical contact is completely forbidden, including holding hands, until after the wedding.

The *shadchan* remains the middleman throughout the *shidduch.* If the date goes well for both parties, the *shadchan* arranges another date. If not, he informs one of the fathers that their child was "very nice" but that the other person didn't think it was a good match. Both parties move on to the next *shidduch* until a suitable match is found.

As an attractive young woman and daughter of a prestigious family, I would have many young suitors who wanted to become part of my family. My parents were not worried about marrying me off. My older sisters had married well, and they thought it would be easy. There was a long line of suitors, so many to choose from and so many good catches. Little did they know (nor I, for that matter), how wrong we all were.

One evening, I came home a little early from school. Mom had a slight smile on her face and I sensed she had some exciting news to share. My little brothers were away at boarding school. My sisters were all married with families of their own. My father was at work as usual.

"Hi Mom, how was your day?" I asked as I sat down for dinner to the delicious London broil she had prepared.

With a slight smile on her face, she announced, "A boy is going to call you tomorrow night at seven o'clock. His name is Nathan. He's smart and comes highly recommended."

Her words triggered a memory: *ten-year-old me walking down a street after some childhood injustice, alone, kicking a rock, and thinking: my parents love me, and I love them, but they will never really understand me or give me comfort. When I'm grown, I will have my own family, and there, I will find love.*

The memory was so vivid, as if I were ten years old again, reliving that moment of temporary defeat, then triumph. *I don't have what I want, but if I wait, it will come.* I had become the queen of waiting. Mostly waiting to die, so I could go to heaven. Every time I experienced a wrong, I would think… *"God will punish them; he'll make it right for me in heaven. Payback time, and rewards for me."* I was also waiting for marriage so I could find comfort. This insight, that had come to me while kicking a rock on that road eight years ago, had sustained me through my childhood. Until this moment, I hadn't let myself believe this magical time would really come, and now I was to have my first date.

In an Orthodox home, a child is material to be molded. Parents were expected to shape them into God-fearing adults. It wasn't personal, or unique to my parents. It was just the way it was.

But now, with marriage, *I* would become an adult. I would find a mate whom I could love and who would love me back, the way I wanted to be loved. What I thought and felt would finally matter to this mysterious husband who would soon be mine. I would be free of my father's house, with its endless rules and rituals. Yes, I would be entering another house of rules and rituals, but we would make that house *our* home, in our image. In our home, children would be allowed to laugh and cry and be heard. I began to smile.

"You're smiling," my mother said, relieved. "That's natural. Dating is exciting."

Was it? I was eighteen years old, but I had never held hands or been in a room alone with a boy.

The next evening, the phone rang at seven o'clock sharp.

"Hello. Is this Laya? This is Nathan. Rabbi Shein gave me your phone number."

"Hello, Nathan. Yes, I was expecting your call."

"Would you like to meet at your house next Sunday afternoon?"

"I would like that very much."

I gave him directions and we hung up. And just like that, my new life had begun.

That Sunday at 5:00 pm sharp, the doorbell rang. While I was upstairs dressing, brushing my hair, and putting on the slightest rouge of lipstick, my father greeted Nathan at the door and showed him to the living room. He guided Nathan to a seat at the table, and my mother brought him a drink and pastries. My mother then waited in the hallway, all the while observing their body language reflected in the mirror.

Our living room was large and well-appointed. One entered through an archway and was met by a full-body reflection in a massive mirror hanging over the wide stone fireplace. A large bay window with fine draperies faced the street. A sofa and matching green upholstered chairs arranged around a marble-topped coffee table provided an entertaining area. In the far corner hung the same crystal chandelier under which the nickel had miraculously dropped onto my brother. Underneath it sat the folding table where my parents and their friends had played card games before it was decided that such conduct had no place in their increasingly fundamentalist home. Now, it was the *shadchan* table.

"What are you studying in school now?" my father asked.

Nathan answered that he was studying a particular chapter in the Talmud. With that, my father got up and walked over to a tall bookcase filled with weighty, oversized religious books bound in reddish-brown leather.

He pulled out the edition Nathan was studying, carried it to the table, and opened it to the given page. Nathan attempted to discuss his field of study and quickly became cognizant of my father's vast Talmudic knowledge. For the next thirty minutes, they talked.

When my father finished his evaluation, he signaled to me in the hallway. I entered the room.

"Laya, this is Nathan," my father introduced us.

Nathan smiled uncomfortably; his face flushed. I immediately felt his embarrassment and rescued him with, "Hi, Nathan."

Then very slowly my father walked out of the room, which had never felt larger. From my position at the *shadchan* table, I could see him lingering in the hallway, hoping to overhear our conversation. I hated this invasion of privacy. I couldn't speak freely or be myself when I knew he was eavesdropping. Nathan and I sat in relative silence until I felt sure that my father had moved on to the kitchen. Then I could relax.

That first date with Nathan was awkward. We were both ill at ease and uncomfortable. I had no idea what to expect or how the time would pass. It was not as though we had met somewhere, found each other attractive, and started a conversation. However, I was pleasantly surprised to find Nathan a tall, fit, handsome young man, refined and mannerly. He was twenty-one and I was his first date, so he was nervous. It was difficult to find conversational momentum.

After a long twenty minutes, Nathan mustered his courage. "Laya, would you like to go out?"

Relieved, I told my parents we were leaving. He escorted me to the rented Chevy he had parked in front of the house, opened the passenger side door for me, and waited for me to sit. It felt uncomfortably close, being alone with him in the car.

I guided him through the back roads to Kennedy Airport and took him to the American Airlines Lounge because it met the religious requirements of being in a public space.

Nathan and I sat at the wide, oval-shaped bar and ordered Cokes, but had nothing to say to one another. Instead, we just stared at what seemed like hundreds of glasses and bottles of wine stacked on the shelves against the wall behind the bar. Liquor bottles with lemons, limes, and red cherries on the counter, savoring a sweet aroma that filled the air and left my mouth watering.

We certainly would not eat anything; the food would not be kosher. Neither one of us knew much about the secular world, so that ruled out most topics of conversation. We were not about to discuss the Talmud, which was mainly for boys, and sports was out of the question. There was no reason to discuss our values, as it was a given that we shared the same ones. Politics were not important, movies were foreign to both of us, and television was a non-entity. So, what was left? We sat in the lounge for two or three hours. He drank his first Coke and ordered another. Mine sat there, slowly going as flat as our evening.

The energy of the airport coupled with the music in the bar, and the waiters serving here and there, compensated for the low energy of our date. Where we sat was an open enclave in the room, indented without a door, so we could see the open airport, hustling and bustling with passengers chatting, walking to and fro, and dragging their suitcases by their sides.

We didn't look like we belonged there: a young, modest girl with a young man in a black suit and a wide-brimmed black hat that never left his head. No likeliness to the other passengers, who were actually there just to travel. It wasn't normal to go to an airport to date someone, but for us, it was perfect.

And as word began to travel in my community that I had been going on dates to the airport, everyone else realized it was perfect for them, too. I set the pace for my generation of religious boys and girls and for generations to come, until 9/11.

At the end of the night, he walked me to the door, and to my great relief, he did not ask to stay. I was glad it was finally over.

My mother was waiting for me inside. "Why didn't you ask him in?"

"The date was over. There wasn't anything more to say."

Monday evening came, and my mother said, "Nathan would like to go out with you again."

"What?" I was so surprised. "Why would he want to go out with me again? It was so uncomfortable! I couldn't wait for it to be over. It wasn't possible for him to have had a good time!"

"He did have a good time and he does want to go out with you again. Can he call you for another date?" My mother was the go-between for my father. "You have to give the boy a chance," my mother continued. "Remember, dating in our culture is different. You don't have much of an opportunity to get to know each other, given our restrictions. In other cultures, you go to the movies, dances, and secular places. Girls and boys hold hands, and we don't."

So I agreed. The next evening at 7:00 pm sharp, Nathan called. This time, I answered directly. I could hear my father pick up the other line in his study, so I quickly set up a time for the following Sunday and we hung up.

We went back to the airport, the same lounge. Nathan's wide-brimmed black hat never left his head. The conversation was a little easier, but I didn't enjoy it or even remember what we might have talked about.

Once again, my mother asked if I had a good time, and like the first time, I said, "Not really, we still struggled for conversation." I was sure he would not call me back and told her so.

When Nathan rang the next evening, I was unprepared. He asked me out again, and of course, I said yes. However, after the third date, I told my mother, "Please, tell the matchmaker I'm not interested in another date with Nathan."

I would receive phone calls from strangers I had never met asking to see me. I knew their names, when they would be calling, and what they would ask. I also knew that I would say yes each time. Then I would coordinate with my father and tell him when the young man was coming. As with Nathan, the same ritual was performed every time.

Were the boys intimidated? Absolutely. Once they figured out that an intense interview would be in store, they took weeks to prepare. My father was unique in our community. To my knowledge, no other fathers put potential suitors through this same screening process. However, it was common in earlier generations in my lineage. When they had daughters of marriageable age, all of my siblings and their spouses adopted this entrance exam.

Any young man who had cleared my father's preliminary hurdles soon realized that prior to our next date he should take a week or two to brush up on his knowledge of the Talmud because my father was going to interview him before I came into the room. If the boy proved less than promising we still went ahead with the date, however, it was understood that he would have no chance of seeing me a second time.

My dating life was completely different from most girls my age. Would a young man simply call on the phone and say, "Hi Laya, this is Saul, would you like to go out on a date?" No.

Where was the spark? The long-awaited stir in me, telling me, *this is the person I want to spend the rest of my life with.* I dated boys of diverse backgrounds in the Orthodox community; some were handsome and some not, some were tall and others short, they were rich and they were poor, high-energy, low-energy... every type of boy one could imagine. And not a glimmer of a spark with any of them. It wasn't extreme wealth or lack thereof, or if he was physically attractive, that meant anything to me. It was only his intellect and a cerebral connection that I needed.

It was not their fault. A boy in his early twenties in our community had missed the opportunity to experience normal boy-girl relationships. They attended boys-only schools and spent most of their days studying. They did not go to dances; they had never held a girl's hand. It was understandable why they lacked basic social skills. Boys in our culture felt deeply intimidated, and in some cases, overly shy. Each time, I tried to be interested and make conversation.

But none of that mattered. Little did anyone know; something had happened that secretly ruined all of their chances.

CHAPTER 13

I WAS 18 YEARS OLD, AND I HAD ACCEPTED A JOB AS A RECEP-tionist at a data processing company, located on the Upper East Side. I loved being surrounded by the neighborhood's beautiful architecture and felt at home in this atmosphere. Our office was down a narrow hallway on the eighth floor of a stately brick building. Past the waiting area was the keypunch room.

The room was full of keypunch machines and their operators, mostly women, entering data all day long. Our clients, who at that time included Hertz Rent-A-Car and Public Broadcast Laboratory, would deliver stacks of papers that were full of raw data: hours worked and rates of pay for payroll, sales, and expenses in a given month, all varieties of business-related information to be reported. Operators would type all of this data into machines which were stacked with 3"x7" cards with 80 columns of numbers 0-9 printed on them.

This was the early stage of computer technology.

When I walked into the offices of General Procedures Corporation, I stepped into my other life.

At work, I was able to continuously grow and succeed. I went from being a receptionist to a bookkeeper to an accountant to a computer programmer, all within six months. I delved into my work, with no commands from my father, learned rabbis, or a higher authority to impede me.

I had expected to have an abrasive, severe boss, like my father, but John was a mild-mannered, courteous man who instantly won over his workforce. A Valley Forge Military Academy graduate who had been an officer in the Armed Forces, he stood tall and straight, head held high, even in the most casual circumstances, exuding confidence and pride. Complementing his muscular build were kind, brown eyes that invited people to approach him. I thought he was handsome, even though at thirty-six he looked older than his age. In the pictures on his desk, his light brown hair was thick and wavy, but it had thinned somewhat in the intervening years. When he caught me looking, he said, "Back then, I wanted to look older. Be careful what you wish for!"

At first, I had no particular attraction to John. Our relationship was simply boss and employee, and he was a good boss. He left me to my own devices and I surged forward, mastering all aspects of the business.

Suddenly the center of my life began to shift. I was developing feelings for John. I don't know when or why they first started; I certainly did not ask for them. Sitting at the reception desk in the mornings, I would hear the turn of the doorknob and feel a rush. *Was it him?* The door would open, I would see John's face, and all at once, I would come alive.

John and I had weekly meetings in his private office to discuss the company's financials. *I wonder if he'll call me into the office today,* I would think, as I hurried from the train station to the office. If he did invite me in, my heart would pound. I felt safe across from him. He was so warm and gentle.

Three months into my time there, we were in John's office with the door closed. This wasn't unusual, as the bustling office prevented us from being able to concentrate and work without interruption when we discussed financial matters.

"Why not move your chair next to mine," he said, "so we can look at the numbers together? We can't pay all the bills today—take a look at this."

I moved next to him, not thinking of anything but the numbers. I always felt at ease in this room.

We discussed the IBM payment which needed to be made and decided to hold off on paying Xerox until the following week.

Without thinking, I laid my hand on John's arm.

The world stopped. A glitch in the firmament. Neither of us breathed.

Such a minor gesture and he made none in return. Yet in his non-response, I felt his tenderness. It was what I liked so much about him, that quiet gentleness and lack of superiority. Even though he was nearly twice my age, he treated me as an equal.

After a moment, we began to breathe again. The world resumed its spinning. I removed my hand. The irretrievable message had been sent and received, almost entirely unconsciously.

Our souls were aligned.

We ended our meeting when all the budgeting decisions had been made, and I simply left the room. Not a word of the enormity of what had happened passed between us. The world began to spin again, just slightly off its axis.

John decided to move the business to a larger office. I was surprised since I didn't think we could afford it.

The next week, we went to the new space to meet with the painters. They noticed that we were standing pretty close to each other. Cracking a knowing smile, the contractor grinned at his buddy, "Standing kinda close, eh?"

John turned crimson and mumbled something.

I recognized his embarrassment, and only then realized how close we were standing. I reluctantly took a step away.

I could not explain even to myself what was happening. It's difficult to articulate how little I knew about the way of the world at the age of eighteen.

I had no idea about the new life that was sneaking up on me because I had no real-world education, no experience, and absolutely no way to understand my relationship with John. What were we? What was I feeling? How could I reconcile it with everything I believed?

The Jewish New Year holidays, *Rosh Hashanah* and *Yom Kippur* kept me away from the office for five days. During those days I thought of little else but John, even though still not a word of recognition had passed between us.

It felt like it had been a lifetime since seeing him as I sat at the Steinberg holiday table, set with a candelabra holding six candles at the center of the table—one light for each child in the family. I was sure my light would betray my surge of emotion. The flame would devour the candle, escape its metal holder, and set the entire table on fire.

But of course, nothing of the sort occurred. Instead, everything proceeded as always, eminently proper and contained.

Dressed in brand new holiday clothes, we sat at our assigned seats marked by our color-coded napkin rings, so we could claim the proper place on the eve of the holiday and then again the following day for lunch. My father rose to recite the *Kiddush*, the blessing on the wine. We stood at our places, motionless, listening to his melodic voice fill the room like an opera singer.

Ordinarily, his chanting could mesmerize a wild beast, but my mind couldn't be swayed from thoughts of John. I imagined him next to me at the table, bowing his head, singing along, something supremely impossible—ridiculous to even imagine. And yet, I so much wanted him by my side, together with my family while we celebrated, I let the image of him with us sustain me through the meal. *Maybe one day? Maybe it wasn't completely absurd?*

I mindlessly passed traditional holiday dishes up and down the table. I dipped apples into honey, symbolic of a sweet new year to come. I nibbled at a small piece of baked fish head, to symbolize our being "at the head of civilization." All the while, I was enveloped in anticipation for what would happen when I returned to the office. I wasn't even imagining a relationship, as I knew nothing of romantic relationships. I just knew that he constantly filled my mind. Something told me it was wrong to feel this way, and yet, I couldn't stop my mind from racing.

Then, the day came. Breathless with excitement, I rushed to the office, and my heart pounded as I stood in the elevator waiting for the doors to part for my floor, anxiously wondering: *Will he feel the same way?*

The instant John saw me, he motioned me into his office. Without a word, he closed the door. I fell into his open arms.

"How I missed you," I whispered in his ear.

"It felt like a century," John said, holding me tight.

After nineteen years on this earth, I had finally learned the meaning of rapture.

CHAPTER 14

OUR EMBRACE WAS THE BEGINNING OF A SECRET LOVE. The feelings swelling within had to be suppressed and not because John was my boss or married with two children. John was not Jewish.

John's wife refused to divorce him, a situation that was common under the divorce laws of the time. Unlike the no-fault divorces of today, back then a person needed a legal reason to request a divorce. John was trapped and miserable, maintaining relative peace for the sake of his children.

His marriage had been in deep trouble from the start. They met on a blind date and when she became pregnant on the first night, his honor told him that he had to marry her for the sake of the child. Now he and his wife, though they lived together, were basically separated, sleeping in separate rooms, and staying together for their two young children. There were many times when I would come to work in the morning and notice that he had extra clothes in the corner of his office. He had slept on his office couch.

It never occurred to me to think of it as a problem. I never intended to take anyone's husband, or even for anything to happen between us besides spending time together. I never dreamed of having an affair, nor did I know what that was. I knew nothing of sex, so how could I recognize sexual desire?

We were companions. Very close companions.

A few weeks into our new shared reality, we held hands for the very first time in public. This chaste touch was a huge escalation from our middle-school-worthy glances and shy smiles. It was exhilarating, scandalous, and wonderful.

As we walked down 58th Street in Manhattan, engrossed in our newfound happiness, Mr. Goldberg, a member of my Orthodox community, turned the corner and came straight toward us. He walked quickly, a newspaper tucked under his arm, his yarmulke centered perfectly on the bald spot of his lowered head.

My heart beat wildly. I froze, unable to even drop John's hand. If Mr. Goldberg looked up, he would catch me in this illicit show of affection.

"What is it?" John asked.

Mr. Goldberg was yards away and closing in fast.

"What's wrong? Oh..." John spotted the obviously Orthodox man almost at our side. He dropped my hand quickly as Mr. Goldberg strode past.

We stood on the sidewalk, not daring to look back.

"He didn't see you. See us. It's okay."

I couldn't speak for the rest of the day.

The next day passed in agony. Then the next, and the next. He hadn't seen us...*right?* Surely if he had, he would have told my parents by now and my relationship, not to mention my entire world, would have crumbled on the spot. We had to be more careful. This just ensured that at the end of our workday, we had to go our separate ways. It was torturous.

"Let's go for one drink," John suggested. For me, this was akin to asking a regular girl to fly off to the Bahamas naked in a hot air balloon. Impossible! Unheard of! But I wanted more time with John away from the formality of the office, as much as he wanted more time with me. Our new discoveries and moments of joy were sullied by guilt and fear. Everything about us was impossible, what more was one drink? We decided to go to the Hilton and thinking back, I can't fathom how my Mother could not detect something amiss. Certainly, she was infatuated with my own father so she knew the signs. For all of this time, she must have simply let it go. It didn't make sense.

Was she giving me the freedom she too wanted?

The hotel bar was dark and filled with constant chatter and clusters of cigarette smoke. As John opened the door for me, I was smacked in the face by the smell of liquor and my head swam with the clamor of patrons laughing and cursing. I was completely out of my element, but still, I went in. I wanted to experience this world, and I felt safe to take the leap with John beside me, who also understood how little I knew. He ordered a Cherry Herring cocktail on the rocks for me.

"Are they real rocks?" I asked John. He smiled.

We settled in the back with our drinks. I sipped my first-ever alcoholic beverage.

My eyes went wide. His eyes softened, and I knew he loved walking beside me in my constant state of discovery.

"Do you like it?" he asked.

It was just the right choice for a first-time drinker, sweet but strong. I savored the drink while gazing wide-eyed at John and gulping in my new surroundings. Every new risk felt like climbing Mount Everest. After this expedition, I would need weeks of recovery before attempting my next feat of courage.

I could *never* explore or uncover parts of me with certain people in my life. John shared my belief in freedom, which no one else in my world could ever understand.

I often grappled with this thought in my mind: how do I measure real freedom? If I act of my own will, then my actions are free, because I determined them independently. But, if my actions are motivated by an *external* authority, like obedience to my parents, or more significantly religious laws, I have then surrendered my autonomy. When this happens, I no longer hear my own voice. But with John, I could feel my voice becoming clearer. For the first time ever, I could take part in philosophical talks where I felt both challenged and affirmed.

He didn't pretend to understand my religion, but he respected it and knew that it would always be a part of me. He sparked a realization in me that there were a multitude of facets within myself that I had never been allowed to explore. He never told me I was beautiful. He may have thought so, but more than anything he considered me to be smart and independent—traits I had earned. That was what he valued in me. This was different from almost every man I had ever encountered.

Despite my joy at stumbling upon such resonance with John, I still had no one else to talk to. How I longed to tell my mother or my sisters what was happening in my soul.

I was delighted when Jenny, my best friend from high school, looked me up. She had also started to work in the city, so we would meet for lunch once a week in the park. The bright sun warmed our backs as we laughed and chatted, like something I had never experienced before. John loved the days I met Jenny. "When you come back from lunch, you can't stop smiling. She makes you so happy."

Jenny and I were like sisters. We always brought the same sandwiches in plain brown bags from our kosher homes: peanut butter on whole-wheat bread. We wore no make-up and sported almost-matching modest skirts and blouses. We laughed about how we had both been brought up the same way: to care about others and live for the next world. We were good, proper Jewish girls. Then, one cool April afternoon she turned to me and said, "Laya, I know it's wrong, but I like my co-worker in the office. His name is Steve. He's Jewish but not religious. I can't tell anyone but you." I almost fell off the wood park bench. I focused on the pigeons across the narrow path while I gathered my thoughts. *Good, perfect, beautiful Jenny also has a secret. Maybe I'm not alone, not crazy. These things happen, and they're natural.* I wanted to jump up, hug her, twirl, and dance! I had found someone to share my sin, my secret, and my truth.

Or...had I? I imagined her shock if I told her about John. After all, he wasn't Jewish, this was an enormous difference in our situations. She was committing a misdemeanor. I was involved in a felony.

"He's married," Jenny went on.

"Oh, Jenny!" I exclaimed, selfishly happy to hear this.

"But he keeps courting me."

To even say those words out loud was shocking. We were so innocent, so blinded by our first flashes of love. Her shining eyes told me that she was enthralled by this new wonder. The rush of feelings had swept us both out of our sheltered lives and into a world so full of hope (and danger). We hardly dared to breathe. She went on.

"We work together all day. It's terrible, Laya! I can't help the feelings that pull at me."

"I know those feelings," I told her, my voice almost a whisper.

Her eyes went wide. "You do?"

I looked around at the trees, the other office workers eating takeout balanced on their knees, the squirrel nibbling a piece of a stolen soft pretzel, and blurted out everything about John. I even told her that he wasn't Jewish, and a wave of relief washed over me. She put her hand on mine and listened, nodding her head empathetically. From then on, our loves were all we talked about, even though we knew they were only dreams.

"Do you think if we lay in the same bed for a whole night, I could still be virginal?" she asked. "Or does God know?"

"God knows everything. But if you only hold each other, and you love each other, how could it be so wrong?" Sharing secrets was something I had never done. Finally, I had a real best friend.

"You guys looked as if you were discussing the fate of the world," John said one day after he had seen us in the park, heads together.

"We were," I told him, more seriously than he could know.

The next week, Jenny was late. When she finally arrived, she had no brown paper bag in hand. She collapsed on the bench and blurted, "Steve's wife is pregnant. He just found out yesterday."

"Oh, that's terrible Jenny," I said.

"No. That's not the terrible part," Jenny responded, tears starting to fall from her beautiful brown eyes. "What's terrible is that he was happy about it. I've never been so humiliated in all my life. I feel like such a fool." She shook with emotion.

Three turbulent months later, Jenny was betrothed to a yeshiva boy the matchmaker had set her up with. They became engaged on the fourth date. I convinced her that it was wonderful and that I was delighted for her. But as for myself, I mourned our friendship. Even though we still spoke, it wasn't the same—and never would be.

"Laya, I'm so happy," she told me.

"That's wonderful." It was hard to hide my disappointment.

"You'll find your yeshiva boy soon," she assured me, misinterpreting my flatness.

Would I? She assumed I would also soon get over John and become a good Orthodox Jewish wife. I wasn't so sure.

When Jenny left, I had no one to confide in. Was she happy now? Should I leave John for a yeshiva boy, so I could also be happy? With no more lunches together, I might never know.

Two weeks after her wedding, Jenny finally called. "I have so much to tell you." She lowered her voice as if we were two schoolgirls telling secrets. "We slept together. It was wonderful. But…"

"But?" I was gripping the phone so tightly my fingers tingled. Did I want this life she now had? Was giving up John worth acceptance in the community?

"Right after making love, he had to leave the bed."

"Why? Where did he go?"

"To the other twin bed across the room."

I sank into my chair. Of course, I knew that my parents slept in twin beds separated by a small table. But I had never thought much about it. I felt deflated. I wanted to hear that Jenny was happy, that she had experienced the romance and intense passion we once whispered about. Instead, she ended up alone in a twin bed. "I bled, Laya. He couldn't stay." She explained the rule. One drop of blood made her impure.

"Didn't you want to lie in bed and have him put his arms around you all night long?" It made me angry, how cold and absolute it was.

"Yes, of course." She lowered her voice even further as if someone might be listening to our conversation.

"But that wasn't the worst part."

I sat back up. "What could be worse than being married, but still sleeping alone?"

"Before the wedding, I had to examine my vagina for seven days with a white cotton cloth."

"Why?" I squirmed, thinking about this obscene violation. It sounded barbaric.

"To make sure that there was no sign of blood. If there had even been a drop, we couldn't have consummated our marriage. And if we weren't sure if the cloth wasn't perfectly clear, we'd have to take it to the rabbi for him to decide."

She described how they would have to take the cloth to the Rabbi in a brown bag. The Rabbi would then take the cloth out of the bag, go to the window, put it up to the sun, and examine the secretion. If he determined that it was not blood, they could have sex on their wedding night. If the Rabbi determined it was contaminated, she would have to start her count of seven clean days all over again, and not consummate the marriage on their wedding night. That also meant that after the wedding, another person had to stay in the house, to ensure that they did not sleep together, until she had seven clean days and went to the *Mikvah* (ritual bath for married women) to officially cleanse herself.

My stomach tightened at the thought of this invasion of her body and her privacy. I imagined them standing in the line to see the Rabbi with a stained cloth in Jenny's bag. What did the other people in line think? Surely, they would know that the couple was there to discuss Jenny's body. It was beyond humiliating, it was shameful and cruel. But I didn't say anything. I wanted to hear more.

"And before the wedding, I went to the *Mikvah*. I had to cut my nails off to my skin, so no dirt could get between my fingernails. Then I had to take a shower, scrub myself with soap, and wash my hair so that I was completely clean. I put on a robe and called the *Mikvah* lady to tell her that I was ready. She took me to the pool and told me to disrobe."

"How awful!"

"I was mortified standing there naked in front of her. She asked me, 'Did you take a shower?' I told her, 'Yes.' She asked, 'Did you wash your hair? Did you wash the soap and the conditioner out? She looked at my nails for any sign of dirt. She checked that I cut my nails and my toenails. She asked, 'Did you wash under your arms and between your legs?'"

"It's so humiliating."

"Yes. I know. I tried to think of God and the holiness of it. I stood in front of her while she examined every part of my body and made sure that there was no dirt or hair left on me. It was hard not to cry, I felt so ashamed."

Did my sisters do this? My mother? Of course, they must. I knew John would love me despite a drop of blood or stray hair. Who was this *Mikvah* lady? Who made these laws?

"I had to recite a prayer and then dunk three times in the sacred pool to make sure that my entire body and all of my hair was underwater. The Mikvah lady watched me, counting. After the third time, I was so glad it was over. I couldn't have done a fourth."

"I couldn't have done any of it." As I said it, I knew it was true.

"It's the law, so I must. If I don't, I could have a bad omen, and something might happen to my child. That would be worse." Her voice was full of fear.

I thought to myself, *how absurd to believe in bad omens. How childish and naive, like believing in fairy tales.*

"At least it's done," I consoled her.

"No, I have to do this every month unless I'm pregnant. Then I get nine months of freedom."

I was not, at this time, aware of any of this.

A woman's existence in Ultra-Orthodox Judaism was controlled by hundreds of laws and regulations. There is even a book of the Talmud, called *Nashim*, meaning "women" or "wives." This is the *most* detailed and extensive of all six books. The male scholars of the community (as women were forbidden Talmudic study) spent centuries engaging in "learned" discussions about the women in their lives. They determined everything imaginable, including the quality and quantity of sex that they were required to give their wives. One finds pronouncements such as "…she on top and him below—this is the way of brazenness; she below and him on top—this is the way of proper intercourse." Time of day, time of the month, position, amount of clothing worn, acts permitted, and acts strictly forbidden were all expounded upon in great detail.

Recently, I had formed a collegiate discussion group that met every Friday night after *Shabbos* dinner with a few college friends and a Rabbi to discuss Judaism. He presented a new topic each week. A few weeks after I spoke with Jenny, the

Rabbi had asked us, "What do you girls think about a woman in our community who misses the *Mikvah*?"

"Who?" a girl asked, her eyes bugging out of her head with salacious curiosity.

"I won't divulge her name, but the *Mikvah* lady told me that this woman hadn't been at the *Mikvah* for four months," the Rabbi revealed.

I was appalled at this discussion. Why was this any of our business? I found it repugnant.

"The question is, is she breaking the law? Or is she running from her husband by not making herself clean for cohabitating together?" the Rabbi continued.

My stomach churned. I refused to participate in this charade, even though the others seemed to enjoy bantering back and forth.

"Gossip isn't holy," I said finally, unable to stand it another minute.

The next week, I disbanded the group. We never met again.

I thought of all the other rabbis and the time they spent discussing women and their bodies, passing judgments, and creating degrading rules. Sure enough, six months later the town gossip was about another woman who was a newlywed, married just a year and a half, and had a six-month-old child. Apparently, she hadn't been to the *Mikvah* since her child had been born. People chattered about how she couldn't count seven clean days or didn't want to, and what was her poor husband to do? How could he bear his lust? We all knew every detail, and it sickened me.

Even though I felt Jenny's humiliation and it angered me, a part of me still believed she must be doing the right thing. I had lived my entire life blindly following laws and rules, terrified of the consequences that might befall me in the afterlife.

It wasn't going to be an easy process to undo a lifetime of brainwashing.

CHAPTER 15

THE WORLD I LOVED STARTED AT 8:10 EACH MORNING.
That's when John and I would meet at the Long Island
Railroad Station at our designated secret spot, on a platform
that was normally abandoned. Without fail, my heart would
flutter each time I saw his face. We could hear the whiz of
distant trains echoing through the air. Our hands found each
other, interlocking as we would walk to the office.

For my 21st birthday, he greeted me with a gold pin,
beautifully designed with my initials engraved on the front. On
the back, John had both of our initials engraved, "JL," along
with that treasured time in our lives, "8:10."

If we went to a store and I commented on something
that I liked, he would show up with it wrapped in a gift box.
Thoughtful gestures like these and displays of affection were
completely new to me.

It was a bone chilly day when we started having breakfast together at Esther's Kosher Dairy, after we met at the train station and before the workday started. This was our attempt at stopping time for a moment. Esther's was a small, plain restaurant. There were no frills or pretty pictures on the wall. The tables were devoid of any centerpieces. They had the basics, and that was it, but John and I created our own ambiance; the physical space was of least importance. Each time I went out with John in public, I felt as if I was starring in my own double-agent mystery novel, and coming here heightened the risk of being discovered.

The mother of one of my high school classmates owned the restaurant and if she had had any inkling of who I was, my world would've shattered on the spot. I felt uneasy every time I walked in. We were the odd couple. John, without a yarmulke on his head, strides into the Kosher deli unaware of the raised eyebrows plastered on the other patrons' faces. And me, modestly dressed, but not literally wearing my religion on my sleeve. No one ever said a word to us, so I can only imagine the thoughts swirling in their minds. "John, I can't sit facing the door or the front window, in case someone sees me," I'd say, and from that moment we arranged ourselves accordingly in public. Always vigilant not to be noticed for fear of retribution.

When we finally arrived at the office, always staggering our entrances, it was business as usual and we set our minds to the tasks of the day.

It was so easy to talk to John; I was calm, fully at ease, and could reveal all my thoughts. One beautiful, warm summer day we had lunch in the park near the Plaza at the UN Building. I began to express my fears and doubts about the world. The ultimatum of heaven and hell had hung over me my entire life and this pressure made me afraid of everything that I did not know. *Why do we exist? What will happen when we die? Is all of this for nothing? What if God isn't real? What if he is?*

As we talked, it started to feel like the park had emptied and we were the only two people there. These were things that normally I could not even think about, let alone tell someone. John wasn't afraid. His rational, self-assured manner allowed me to dive deeper into feelings that normally would have overwhelmed me. My fears did not disappear, but I suddenly felt safe. As I continued to confide in John, my fears started to loosen their grip and feel a bit farther away.

Safety is not a strong enough word for the new existence that we had uncovered together. It did not matter that we only had fleeting moments together: pause time, meeting points, discrete meals, glances in the office...we had slowly built our own little world, just by being together. I knew that we could never get married, but still, I wanted to stay in our world forever.

Alone in the park, we sat without an inch separating us on a secluded bench. With each glance into each other's eyes, we both felt the tension and I could feel my desire rising. This was a world outside of the reality I knew. Our eyes met, then our lips.

Most girls begin their sexual awakening in high school, but at 21, I was still inexperienced. As I crossed into forbidden territory, my heart began to pound intensely.

My mind knew this was wrong, but my heart came to a different conclusion. This was a celebration, an expression of our love. *Could this be the meaning of life? If so, it's worth living for.*

Even as I fell more deeply in love with John, at home I dutifully continued to meet one potential suitor after another. One weekend, I went to the flower show three times on three separate but equally boring dates. For months after, the sight of a budding rosebush made me shudder. It became known among the *yeshiva* boys that I was a tough catch, and unbeknownst to me, I had become a kind of Holy Grail.

They were on a hopeless quest.

Still, my father kept arranging dates with infinite patience, making my weekends away from John even more unbearable. On Monday mornings at Esther's Dairy, finally reunited, I would recount to John the tedious dates I had endured that weekend. He took my hands in his and stared into my eyes. "If I were dating you, I would climb the walls to get to you. I would never give up. I would plant myself outside your door and wait until you said yes."

"But my father would never say yes."

"That's why I wouldn't ask him," John said. "I would ask you."

A shudder of fear—and joy—traveled down my spine. Was it really that simple?

I thought to myself, *this can't go on—just a few more months and I'll end it.*

Yehuda, another one of my suitors, had fallen instantly in love with me. He was tall and confident, the only son of a wealthy man.

I was too caught up in my own relationship with John to think of Yehuda's feelings. He was merely an obstacle to get through until I could return to work and John on Monday. So of course, I asked my mother to put a stop to the dates after the first one.

Denying Yehuda was the final straw.

The next day, my father summoned me into his home office. "Yehuda's father called me directly. He went around the matchmaker, and he is not that kind of man. He is begging you to give it another chance."

"I can't…"

He held up a hand.

"I told him no. But he kept begging: 'Yehuda wants one more date. He's sure he just needs *one* more time to be with you and he *knows* it will work.'"

My father stared at me, as though if he looked hard enough, he would find an answer to this perplexing riddle.

"His father is begging me. What do you say? Give him one more chance?"

"No, I'm sorry, but he's not for me." I felt sick to my stomach, but I knew I would never marry Yehuda, so what was the point? It would only hurt him further.

My father's eyes opened wide with anger. "This isn't like you. You're usually so sweet, so kind."

Did my father care about Yehuda, or did he see something in the desperation of Yehuda's father that resonated with his own? This had been going on too long. Wasn't he just as anxious for the match to work?

Whatever his motivation, that night, he called me into the living room. "Sit down," he commanded, pointing to the green velvet couch in front of the windows.

I sat.

He pulled a chair from the dating table right up to me and sat on it. He inched the chair closer, closer, as close as he could get without our knees touching. So close, I could feel his breath on mine and had to hold my own. I felt like a mouse caught in his trap. He studied my face, breathing hard as he allowed his anger to grow like an approaching storm. He leaned in and said, "I can't understand why I have not found a husband for you. It's been almost four years! Your sisters took just a few months."

I didn't speak. What could I say?

My silence made him angrier. His voice rose, with every word. "What are you doing? Why are you wasting your life away? What do you do at work every day? What is it all for? Work, work, work. All for nothing. What's wrong with you?"

He hurled his words at me. "Do you want to be like your cousin Shani? Never married? She just has a career and is unhappy. What does she have? Zilch. Nothing to speak of for herself. No husband, no children, nothing! She's just a lonely spinster with a career. What a failure. Is that what you want for yourself? Do you want to have nothing? Why are you so stubborn? Do you know what the Torah says about stubbornness? *Do not be like the horse or the mule. God will guide His children, but if we become stubborn that can lead to making bad decisions in life.*"

On and on he went, making threats and quoting scripture.

Finally, it was over. He shoved back his chair and stormed away, leaving me alone, stiffly poised on the edge of the seafoam green couch.

I hadn't uttered a word.

Our green couch "discussions" became a recurring event. Each lecture was longer and harsher than the last. I never said anything. I sat, staring straight ahead, and waited for it to be over. I held my breath and my tongue. I knew that the only way to reach the end was to withstand it, sitting quietly and respectfully, never daring to contradict, never attempting to explain. After all, I couldn't tell him the real reason I wasn't falling for the yeshiva boys. His head would have exploded right there in the living room. He would have expired on that same dreaded couch.

After our sessions, my mother tried to reassure him, to restore harmony. "She's looking for someone extraordinarily special."

That was true, but I had already found him.

CHAPTER 16

J OHN AND I HAD BEEN TOGETHER FOR FOUR YEARS. After coming home from an ordinary day of work, everything seemed normal. I hung my coat in the women's closet and washed my hands in the bathroom. I recited the blessing on my way to the kitchen, where my mother was waiting with my hot dinner.

"Laya," she said. But she didn't turn from the stove.

I heard something ominous in her tone. I watched my mother set down my dinner in front of me. I waited.

She sat down across from me, her face grave. "Your father would like to come by your office tomorrow and see it for himself. He would like to meet your boss."

Nausea washed over me. And not because a grown woman's father coming into her office to meet her boss was supremely inappropriate and strange, I knew John would understand, and I didn't care what anyone else thought. The image of my father and John together made me ill. It was as impossible as John and I marrying. The two worlds couldn't interact. It was as dangerous as planets spiraling out of their orbits.

"Okay," I managed, placing my napkin on my lap and avoiding her eyes. I could barely swallow, forcing the food in my mouth down. *Did she know? Did someone see us? Report us?* No, that was impossible. If that had happened, my father would already be here, berating me. But they must have some suspicion, or else why would my father come?

"I'm not hungry, Mom.." I tossed and turned all night, unable to sleep. I told myself that my father just wanted to know what I was doing in the office all day, he wasn't interested in John. But then I would close my eyes and imagine my father saying to my mother, "What could the attraction be? Something isn't normal and I'm going to find out what it is."

Would he make me stop working at the office?

And then what would I do?

The morning after I was informed of my father's planned visit, I met John at the train station and tried to prepare him.

"We're both grown men. He doesn't intimidate me."

My father walked through the glass doors of our front lobby an hour later. John greeted him with a strong handshake, which my father returned in kind. I remembered the first time I had met John and how taken aback he had been by my own firm handshake. "Who taught you how to shake hands?" he asked after the interview.

"I never knew there was any other way."

"Have a seat, Mr. Steinberg," John offered. They sat down at John's desk and began to converse, out of my range of hearing.

I sat at my desk and pretended to work, my heart in my throat. I counted the seconds, each one longer than the one before. *What am I doing here? How did I allow this to happen?*

Finally, after what felt like a century, John rose. *Thank God it's over. What should I do? What should I say?* Somehow, my father left the office, and I began to breathe again.

"Your father is an interesting man. He has a strong business sense," John said to me after he left.

"What?"

"Your father, I admire what he's accomplished."

I sat in shock at John's relaxed demeanor, surprised that the world continued to turn.

That night, I went home to my mother's hot dinner. She put my food on the table and sat across from me.

"Your father did not like your boss."

Little more was said. I was used to not disclosing my emotions and true thoughts to my mother. The mask I donned to disguise my discomfort at the entire situation was firmly rooted, but the terror that gripped me inside felt like a tightly drawn corset that got tighter with each breath I attempted to take. It took me an entire month to calm down. John tried to assuage my fears with reason.

"He hasn't done anything," John said. "He hasn't even spoken to you. Besides, he doesn't have to like me, only to respect me."

And, the most convincing argument of all: "Your father is losing control of you and he knows it. He came here hoping to find something truly terrible, so he could take you back. But he only found me, and I wasn't the monster he expected. Now, he doesn't know what to do."

If my father's faculties hadn't been clouded by rage he would have noticed, and it would have been the end. If my mother had been the one who visited, she would have caught sight of John's photo on the shelf adjacent to my desk, which I had forgotten to remove. She had been madly in love with my father at my age. She knew the signs. But she hadn't visited, so that day I got away with it.

But I knew our secret couldn't last. I felt the walls closing in on us. I was still under their rule, both emotionally and practically. They knew something was going on, they just didn't know exactly what.

Were they following me?

How could they not know?

Surely, the end was near.

CHAPTER 17

"I FEEL GUILTY EVERY TIME WE TOUCH EACH OTHER. I'M not allowed to touch a man until my wedding night."

John and I were intimate in other ways, such as holding hands, kissing, and embracing, which would seem tame to the women who fully participated in the sexual revolution. But for me, it was forbidden, even sinful. "My religious upbringing prohibits this behavior. I'm not allowed to touch a man until my wedding night."

"*Our* wedding night," John said.

"Impossible."

"It's the only way."

But it wasn't. Not in my mind. There was only one actual way for our relationship to end. *This was the last time. I'm never going to go further than this. Just a few more months and I'll gather up the courage to leave him, and everything will be okay.*

Aside from small moments before and after work, John and I never had the ability to be alone together. I had no way to explain any long absence to my parents. I told myself that our romance would come to an end, and soon. At least we should make the most of this time before it was over. I came up with the idea to say that I was staying at Jenny's so that we would be able to stay at a hotel for the night.

Recently, we began stopping at the Waldorf Astoria's Peacock Alley restaurant for breakfast before work. John always enjoyed a full meal, while I just drank coffee as it was the only kosher item on the menu. It had become *our* hotel, another place where we could slip into our own world. It was thrilling to be able to spend a night there together, just the two of us.

I had never booked a hotel room, much less slept in one. The entire idea was frightening. I loved Waldorf's storied grandeur and its international clientele.

It was the most beautiful hotel in America. Dignitaries from all over the world stayed there. Two doormen opened the double doors lined with gold, and a white and black marble floor leading to the hotel lobby. The first thing you noticed was the gold staircase and velvet carpet on the steps that went up to the mezzanine floor. The decor was regally decorated in red and gold velvet.

I confirmed it with Jenny. "If my mother calls me at your house, tell her I'm in the bathroom and then call me right away. My room number is 402."

"Okay. But I'm nervous," she said. "I hope she doesn't call."

I knew she would call and I was terrified. The morning would bring bliss or disaster.

I'm sure I was much more afraid than the other people in the hotel having actual affairs. The funny part was that our night was probably also the most innocent.

All night, John and I held each other, lying together in the cool air on the spacious king-sized bed. He stroked my face ever so gently as he whispered, "I love you so much. I can't live without you."

I kissed his neck, his chest, and his back. His muscular, smooth body was angelic.

The phone's ring jolted me out of my blissful reverie. It was Jenny.

"Your mother called looking for you!" I bolted out of bed and scrambled to the phone.

"Sorry, Mom. I was in the bathroom." My brain was racing—my heart pounding. We continued to chit-chat about the day. After a few moments, we hung up.

"We can't go on like this forever," John said.

He was right, but not in the way he thought.

Just another few months, and I'll end this, I told myself.

CHAPTER 18

THERE WERE FINANCIAL ISSUES IN JOHN'S COMPANY THAT had long been ignored. In a way, they were a taboo subject. John was a terrific salesman and knew how to bring in blue-chip accounts. But he was unwilling to fire employees who were not performing and make other difficult choices that all business owners face.

In 1972, he merged the company with a data processing firm in Mineola, Long Island, and became an executive of the company. He was given thirty percent ownership. The other two partners did not want any redundancies, which meant his employees, including me, would not be part of the new enterprise. They had a full staff of their own. We were both devastated, but there was nothing we could do about it.

I accepted a position with the IT department at MasterCard, where John had a contact. I was the only female of twenty-three computer programmers. Opposition from some of the men was palpable. As always, I put my head down and worked. I took my job very seriously. I was motivated to delve deeper into computer programming and learn more about cutting-edge techniques to improve my skills and be a valued asset. I asked for more projects. Meanwhile, the other programmers did the bare minimum. They were motivated to play chess with the IT Department's chess club and mock MasterCard's customers for paying such high-interest rates. MasterCard was my first lesson in corporate waste.

I observed that MasterCard didn't need so many programmers, most were ballast. Only six of us were doing the job.

Management said to me, "You'll never be able to do it." We tried and no one was able to tackle this. We would love to be the first company to tackle this. We were; I figured it out in one day. For me, it was simply because I was focused and logical. I wrote the very first computer program to separate first, middle, and last names on the customer database. MasterCard became the first company with computer technology to send a computerized letter to a customer that began with, *Dear Mr. Jones,* instead of, *Dear John H. Jones, or simply, Dear John.*

The programming manager was so impressed, he told me that I was to be promoted to supervisor after the upcoming holidays. I swelled with pride. I realized I had made a real contribution to technology.

Not long after, the Vice President of programming invited me to play chess with the group. I made an unforgivable mistake: I won the match.

The group of programmers laughed and teased. "Well, Joe, who knew you would be beaten by a girl? Soon she's going to be your boss!"

I had made my first enemy.

My second antagonist was my supervisor, Lenny. He was married but wanted to begin an affair with me. I was completely oblivious to his overtures. He invited me to meet him for a tennis game after work. I loved tennis and was always looking for a partner. This time, though, I wouldn't be so stupid as to beat a superior.

"Sure, I'd love to," I said. I thought I had it all figured out: we would play doubles, and I would play on Lenny's team. I invited Jerry, another programmer who played, to find a partner and join us.

Not a soul showed up. I waited till six, then left, confused. The next day, I found Lenny.

"Why didn't you meet me at the tennis court?

"Why did you invite Jerry," he responded. Anger and hurt filled his eyes.

I couldn't understand what he was getting at. "I thought it would be more fun to play doubles."

He walked away. I called Jerry, the other programmer that I had invited to play doubles.

"Why didn't you show up at the tennis court?"

"Lenny was mad that you invited me."

I was so naive, I had no idea what was going on behind my back until I returned to work after the Jewish holidays, thinking I was about to be promoted.

The manager called me into his office. Full of excitement, head held high, I went to accept my promotion.

"I'm sorry, but I have to let you go."

My heart skipped a beat. "Let go? What for? Why?"

"Lenny went over my head. He told my boss that every Friday, after lunch, instead of going home early, as you requested, to prepare for the Sabbath, you meet a man at the Union tennis courts. The other programmers said it was true. It's too late, there's nothing I can do about it now. They're all against you. It's really better if you just go."

Even the people I thought were my friends at the office wouldn't return my calls. A new part of the business world had revealed itself, but it didn't completely shock me. Getting cheated out of a promotion, a job, a spot on the local baseball team, or the option to become a Torah scholar was par for the course in my life. I accepted this sort of discrimination because as a woman in Orthodox Judaism, I was always second-class. My place in the world was as a mother, a daughter, and a wife, and anything else was secondary.

I would look for a new job.

John had a better idea. "We should diversify our business. Let's buy the print shop around the corner from my new office." John was a risk-taker and always thinking about acquiring new ventures.

"But I don't know a thing about printing," I protested.

John sounded so convincing and, at the time, I was still sure that he was a good businessman. After all, he had successfully lured many Fortune 500 companies to move over and become clients at his own data processing company when he left IBM.

John didn't have funds for a downpayment on the print shop, so I took the money out of my savings, and we'd pay the rest over two years.

Suddenly, at twenty-three years old, I had become a small business owner, unbeknownst to my parents.

This print shop was a part of my growth and becoming a more skilled businessperson. I loved helping customers design their wedding invitations and birth announcements. Every type of person walked through the door, from the wealthiest to the poorest. And since there were no Bar Mitzvah invitations being sent in Oyster Bay, Long Island, John and I could exist in this community without fear of exposure. It was our safe zone.

I started my first company, Time Sharing Corporation in the same town. TSC brokered mainframe computer time to smaller data processing companies who could not afford their own computers.

From those profits, I was able to purchase my first used car. I was thrilled. It was a yellow Corvair with a black convertible top. The problem was that my car was a stick shift and didn't know how to drive it. John taught me how to drive the Corvair. "You'll be able to drive any motor vehicle once you master the stick shift."

Six months into juggling the two companies, just as my mother and I were finishing dinner, my father came home.

"Just a small dinner tonight. We have a lot of paperwork," he told my mother. She always helped him with the paperwork for his business but when she wasn't there, I would have to take over. I felt sorry for my mother, but that meant I was free for the night.

The telephone in my father's office rang.

"I'll get it, Morton." My mother started for the office, but a second ring never came.

"Strange," she said.

It was my signal. It wasn't strange to me. As I expected, the office phone rang again, just once. I excused myself and went upstairs to my parent's bedroom, my heart pounding in fear. I sank down between their two twin beds, where the home telephone sat on the nightstand. Then I waited and listened, fighting the fear building inside me. Luckily, my father ate quickly. I listened for the scraping of his chair, their footsteps into the office, then silence.

I had to wait until they were in the office, where the phone was on a different line. I dialed one number at a time, my hand shaking, and strained to listen for footsteps or the click of someone picking up the receiver downstairs in the kitchen, the only other extension.

John picked up on the first ring.

I whispered, "Hi."

I could almost feel his relief through the phone line. He would never speak first, in case somehow it wasn't me. "Hi, sweets. Are you okay?"

"I'm fine, but I don't like calling from here. What's wrong?"

"Will you marry me?" John asked. "I want an end to all of this. I want to marry you and be together forever. Now. No more waiting."

I was dumbfounded. *I cannot marry John, but I **can't not** marry him. The time is right, but the marriage is wrong. It's up to me, but nothing is up to me. I cannot possibly decide, but it is my problem to resolve. I am a twenty-four-year-old woman crouching in fear on the floor of my parent's bedroom. How long can this go on? What am I to do? I don't know what to do. Am I weak? Am I foolish? Am I smart? Am I courageous? Oh, what am I, who am I—what am I to do?*

Then suddenly, I realized, *John will make it all right.*

I surrendered.

"Yes, I will." The words just came out and I relinquished myself to him.

"I love you. I will care for you. You will be mine," he whispered back to me.

The wheels were set in motion. John and I were not the types to watch things happen and then wonder why. We *made* things happen. It was in our DNA.

John filed again for divorce, but his wife would still not agree to it. The only alternative was to head to Nevada, the first state in the country to pass no-fault divorce legislation.

It was a time of deep inner reflection for me. I knew in my soul that his circumstances were not the same as Jenny's lost love. I also knew how my situation sounded: he was almost 18 years my senior, married, with a daughter in college, just five years younger than I was. But that did not alter a profound reality. We were two people, who against all odds, found love. Life is never black and white.

While I kept our businesses running in Long Island, John moved to Reno and secured a computer programming job at Nevada University. After six weeks of living and working there, the State of Nevada would consider him a resident and would authorize a divorce. Once the courts had finalized it, he would be free to marry me.

The first thing on my agenda every morning was to rush to the post office to pick up my letter. His letters sustained me for the weeks we were apart. I would reread the day's letter before I hit the pillow each night and then hide it under my bed. We wrote about the business and how much we missed each other, counting the days in each letter until our reunion.

After six interminable weeks, John presented his petition to the court.

The State of Nevada granted him the divorce.

Again and again, I considered telling my mother or my sister of my decision. But I never uttered a word to anyone because of an ominous phone call I had received one year earlier.

"Hi Laya. It's Sarah, do you remember me? We were in the same class at Beth Jacob High School?"

"Sarah, hi." I was confused. Why would she contact me after so many years?

"I was told that you weren't married. I'm not either. Do you have time to talk?"

I realized then why I didn't recognize her voice. It had changed. The girl I knew from math class was bubbly, outgoing, and full of confidence. This person on the other end of the line sounded frightened, her voice low and trembling.

"I'm locked in my parents' house," she whispered.

I couldn't believe it. I tried to process her words.

"Two years ago, I fell in love with a married man from Lakewood. He has three children and a wife, but he wants a divorce. We're both religious, but we want to get married. We're in love with each other." Her voice was desperate. "The Rabbis forbade him a *Get*."

A *Get* is the religious version of a civil divorce. Without that document, men and women were not free to remarry.

"We want to start a life together, and my parents heard rumors we might run away. So they shut me in. I haven't been able to call anyone. But then I heard about you. Since you're also single, I thought there might be a reason for that, and I always felt that you were understanding." She was hopeless and in despair. I wondered how she had gotten my number.

How I wish I could help her, but what could I do? "They can't lock you up!" I was incredulous.

"But they can. I'm trapped until I swear to give him up. He and his family must move away to a place unknown to me."

Now she was weeping. I had no idea what to do. I couldn't confide in her. I barely knew her. I had no idea how else I could help her. What was she asking of me? Even if I called the police, she would never testify against her parents or the law of the community.

She needed a friend on her side, and I wished we could share our predicaments. But I knew that even though her own parents had imprisoned her—a grown woman!—against her will, she still wouldn't side with me being with John. The man she loved was Jewish. I didn't have that luxury.

As she went on with her story, it became clear to me that my parents could also lock me away if they ever found out about John. We had to be more careful than ever.

"I'm so sorry," I told her. "I wish I could help you." I hung up the phone with a heavy heart.

Sometimes, I wonder what happened to Sarah. But the differences between us made further contact impossible. I was terribly sad for her. A secular divorce from the state court would not be valid to them. In their minds, without a religious divorce, they would-be adulterers. As for Sarah and myself being friends, she could never condone my relationship with a non-Jewish man. She would be shocked at my actions and, she too would shun *me*. There was nothing I could do but learn from her situation and try to protect myself.

PART II

Exodus

CHAPTER 19

THE NIGHT BEFORE I LEFT FOR RENO, I PULLED MY BRAND new '73 silver Ford Pinto into the garage so no one would see the red suitcase in the backseat. Packing the suitcase had been no easy task. Each morning, I sneaked a shirt or a pair of shoes into the office, until I had everything I needed.

Now that everything was set, from the master plan to the plane ticket, the enormity of the moment began to sink in. Anxiety gripped me. My family wasn't just losing me, they were also taking on a full load of embarrassment, shame, and pity from a community that excels at dishing out all three. People would be shocked. This was the perfect family. I had been everyone's Laya. How could this have happened?

I steeled myself. *Stop thinking. Just do it.*

I fished for my gloves and closed the garage door. The cold December air helped me to clear my thoughts.

I walked into the house I had always called home and never would again. As I pushed open the back door to the kitchen, a wave of sadness came over me. My mother was in the kitchen, reading the *New York Times*. The pages crackled. The wall clock ticked.

All was still, but never tranquil. Not in this house. The tension generated by my father's incessant demands was shown in the small creases around her eyes. Her face would light up when she saw me. I brought life to this house and light to her life. Leaving would be easier if I didn't love her so much.

What will happen to her without me? Who will bring her flowers every Friday for the Sabbath?

A few years earlier, my mother had asked me to accompany her to the hospital for a mysterious surgery. Of course, I agreed.

My mother would not even consider telling me the details about her illness, or even name the illness itself. It was a matter of protecting me from the harsh realities of life. She didn't want my spark of youthful excitement to dim just because her hopes for splendor, excitement, and possibility were gradually extinguishing.

My father had a fear of sickness, doctors, and hospitals, so he stayed far away. He had not accompanied her on any of the doctor visits, nor did he accompany us to the hospital, or visit her after the procedure.

With me by her side, the operation seemed to go fine. But I was young and unaware. Much later I realized that I should have researched her condition and conferred with my sisters to make all of us more knowledgeable.

We were all accustomed to accepting the word of authority, in this case, that of the doctor, without question.

The doctors gave my mother medications and a recovery plan. I had no idea what my mother was going through. Nor was I informed that the lump the doctors removed from her breast had turned out to be cancerous. I followed my mother's silent lead and took care of her as lovingly as I could.

She heard me enter the kitchen and spun around with a warm smile that pierced my heart. "Laya! You're home late. I left some dinner for you. Would you like me to heat it up? It will just take five minutes. It's a nice steak."

"No thanks, Mom. I'm not hungry."

She smiled at me for an endless moment, then went back to her paper. She wasn't surprised by my response. It had become a nightly ritual. I was rarely hungry after work, and tonight of all nights, nothing could get down my throat. Still, my mother lovingly made me dinner every single night. I had asked her to stop. I hated for her to go through all that trouble, but she wanted to.

Caring for me gave her purpose.

My stomach knotted. I was disloyal to this woman I admired above all others. She was so intelligent, so dedicated to being a God-fearing woman. She heeded all the laws handed down from the Lord. She wanted to be worthy of The World to Come by blindly obeying God's commandments.

And worthy she was.

How I didn't want to hurt her! Sadness filled my heart. I knew she would find no small glimmer of sunlight in this darkness. By now, of her own volition, she had become as religious as my sisters. Guilt and superstition permeated her being. Although she disliked many traits of the ultra-religious, she joined them completely. She believed in sacrificing everything to God.

She will get over it. In time, she will move on just like the others. We will lead different lives.

I crept quietly down the hallway toward the stairs, doing my best to avoid attracting my father's attention. He sat at the head of the dining room table, surrounded by volumes of the Talmud. As usual, he was engrossed in his studies.

While I was overwhelmed with emotion for my mother, toward my father I felt numb. I had never been comfortable alone with him. Now, in this moment of great inner turmoil, instead of being able to come to him for advice I was reduced to sneaking and lies.

I locked my bedroom door even though it wasn't necessary. My mother would never have entered my room without knocking. She trusted me. Why shouldn't she? I never did anything wrong. My father never dared to enter my room because I was a girl. The only exception was on the eve of Passover.

With my mother trailing behind, he would inspect my closet and desk drawers for *hametz* (leavened bread), which was not allowed in the house during Passover. It was a ritual performed with a candle and a feather to sweep away the slightest crumb; they didn't really expect me to be stashing loaves of rye.

While searching through my drawers for *hametz*, my mother saw the pocket watch. "Did you buy that pocket watch? Who is it for? Your boss?"

I was dumbfounded. Yes, I had bought the watch for John. It was clearly a man's watch. I was saving it for his birthday. *Why did I leave that watch in my drawer? What's wrong with me? I must be crazy.*

Somehow, I shrugged and answered sheepishly, "Oh. That? I'm saving it." Meanwhile, my heart was pumping madly. I prepared for the worst.

But my father was so consumed with his mission to find *hametz*, that he didn't even hear my mother's question. He was so busy trying to brush away every crumb of non-existent bread that he missed the enormous, shiny hunk of *hametz* sitting in plain sight.

It baffles me even today that my mother accepted this lame response as if it made sense. Nothing more was said.

As they left the room to go to the next, I collapsed on my bed, clutching the pocket watch in my palm.

I wrote two copies of two letters—one to mail and one to keep so I could remember exactly what I had written. I addressed the first letter to my parents. The second to Candice. I folded them into my purse. Then I showered, laid out my clothes for the morning, set my alarm for five a.m., and attempted to sleep, the last night I would spend in my childhood bed.

I stared at the hands on the clock, watching them edge closer and closer toward my freedom.

The alarm buzzed me from my slumber. It was December 3, 1973, three months after Israel's Yom Kippur War and one week before the Hanukkah holiday. I put on the clothes I had laid out and went to the linen closet. I assumed my disappearance would cause enough of a commotion in the family that the house would be full of people, and someone would certainly need to use my bed. Since I was already being a burden, I felt bad making one of my sisters change the sheets. I remade the bed and put white notepaper on top of the spread, which read: *Clean Sheets.*

Years later, my brother told me that my family took my odd note to be either a grave insult, a sign of insanity, or proof that John had manipulated me and I wasn't myself.

I looked at my spotless bedroom one last time, the only private space in my adult life. The deep blue carpet matched the ocean a mile away. The baby blue walls matched the sky. Some days felt like floating, others felt like sinking. This was my safe harbor in all the storms, where I would escape my father's controlling eye. This is where I would pray for my family, for myself, and for John.

I stepped into the hall and closed the door behind me.

The house felt empty even though I knew my parents were asleep behind their closed doors. My siblings were all married or away at boarding school. Where it was once filled with children and bustling with excitement, now it felt deserted and lonely.

I crept down the stairs.

I rested my things on the kitchen table, put on my winter coat, and wrapped a scarf around my neck. Gently picking up my things from the table, I slowly unlocked the door and slipped out.

I did not look back.

My Pinto roared to life in the otherwise silent morning. My pulse matched its pace as I reversed out of the driveway. This late autumn morning was especially cool, and when dawn washed the darkness from the sky, I knew it would be a beautiful day, the biggest of my life.

Still in a daze, I arrived at John's office, where I worked while he was away in Reno. I went straight into the computer room, soaking in the familiar adrenaline rush. I needed this feeling. Massive machines purred with quiet efficiency in the two-thousand-square feet of air-conditioned space. I moved from machine to machine, typing in commands, punching out 50,000 cards on the IBM Punch Card Tabulating machine, and then sorting them on an IBM Card Sorter in the proper inventory sequence. How I loved that sound!

At my advanced age, I was supposed to be married with five children, running a household with a baby in one arm and dragging a toddler with the other. I should already have created the perfect home for a husband who sat in a *Kollel* (yeshiva for married men) and studied Torah all day long.

Instead, I was running massive scientific machinery because I understood the sheer logic of it. In addition to running my own small business, I considered myself a computer expert at the infancy of computers. My work life thrilled me every single day. Normally I never wanted to leave that room, but today I had a more important project.

I got back in the Pinto and drove to that familiar spot of endless failed dates and uncomfortable silences, JFK Airport. Now I was finally here for myself.

I checked in, then called my mother. I didn't want to, but I called her every day and if I had missed the call, she would have been concerned. Thankfully, the glass phone booth insulated our conversation from the public-address announcements.

"Your sister wrote to you from Montreal," she said.

"Read it to me," I said. "Please."

I knew I would never see that letter, and I wanted to hear about Marilyn and my three young nieces one last time. As she read, a pall of wretchedness came over me. I struggled to hold back my tears. I couldn't let my mother hear me cry. My sisters were dear to me, and I would never see them again.

I loved them fiercely but was unaware that I, too, was loved in return.

I can't explain it, but I didn't know they cherished me in the same way that I cherished them. I never thought I was important, so I never thought, as crazy as it might sound, that I would be missed. I believed each person lived their own lives, and as I was about to marry the forbidden, they would write me off. They would move on with their own spouses and children, erasing me from their minds.

Had I known how my leaving would affect them, I would have hung up that phone and gone directly home, not able to bear the pain I would cause.

I stole a look at my watch. Ten minutes until boarding. "Read it again," I begged, trying to keep the emotion out of my voice.

"Okay, Mom," I said when she had finished. "Bye."

CHAPTER 20

T HE COURTHOUSE WAS HUMMING WITH ACTIVITY. NERVOUS couples sat in rows on hard wooden chairs. The rest of the chamber was just as uninviting. As we joined them, I couldn't help thinking of how different my wedding was supposed to be.

The joyous, extravagant marriage celebrations of my Orthodox royal family were steeped in millennia of tradition. Before the ceremony, I would have sat atop a lace chair as four hundred guests paid joyous tribute.

At the reception, male guests would have somersaulted through the air in elaborate dances. Women would have shyly peeked through the lattice wall that separated them from the men, who were forbidden to even glance their way. We would have feasted on a lavish smorgasbord ordered by my father; the head of our family, pillar of the community, and wise man of the synagogue.

Every moment of the proceedings would be determined by an ancient ritual that was performed in service of the glory of God as channeled through the generosity of my father.

Panic set in. What if the judge wouldn't marry us? I was twenty-five, but I looked sixteen. John was forty-three. Strangers always assumed that he was my father, which was embarrassing for both of us. Now, though, we might have a real problem.

John sensed my fear. "What is it?" he asked.

"What if the judge says we're not allowed to get married because I'm too young?"

"But you're twenty-five."

"The judge won't believe my age. What if he calls my parents to ask permission?" That I, a twenty-five-year-old woman, thought this was a possibility spoke to my extreme ignorance of the secular world.

I was raised in a world of absolute authority: the Rabbi, the Talmud, my father, my God. Our community was dedicated to disciplining the tiniest infraction. Eyes were everywhere to report too-short skirts or the consumption of forbidden foods.

It took all my will not to run out of that waiting room. In an instant, all the freedom, promise, and safety I had felt since our first embrace had evaporated. I was a child again, suffocating in my father's tightly controlled domain. I wouldn't have been the least bit surprised if my father walked into the room, yanked me out of my chair, and led me away while the people around me clapped and whistled.

John said, "We're thousands of miles from your family. They can't reach you here. Plus, it doesn't matter what anyone thinks."

Such simple words were revolutionary to me. In my world, what other people thought was all that mattered. To go against the community was the ultimate shame.

In the next few days, my family would not only lose me but the respect of the community. I felt the shame flow through me—then out. I was with John. I was safe. I was about to create my own home, one filled with unrestricted love, not hindered by a burdensome duty to God, a home where I could be free.

The bailiff called our names. We walked hand-in-hand, heads held high, to a small room where a judge in a black robe sat on his dais. "Do you, Laya Steinberg, take John Martinez to be your lawfully wedded husband? In good times and in bad..."

"I do."

"And do you, John Martinez, take Laya Steinberg to be your lawfully wedded wife? In good times and in bad..."

"I do."

"By the power vested in me by the state of Nevada, I pronounce you husband and wife."

It was done.

I was no longer afraid.

Yet I was still anxious to hurry out before the judge could change his mind.

On the way back to the hotel, we found a small mailbox. John held my hand as I dropped in the letters to my parents and Candice, releasing them along with centuries of tradition and twenty-five years of love and anguish. It all disappeared into the black with a soft swish.

Later, John and I would consummate our marriage in the traditional sense. But this act of releasing those letters into darkness was the first consummation. The last drops of terror were gone.

There was no turning back.

Dearest Parents, Mom and Dad,

As I write this letter to you, I cry bitter tears. What I am doing will, no doubt, hurt you in many ways. First, let me tell you that I do now and have always loved you both dearly. Nothing in my upbringing caused this, and

I can still say, "Ani Ma-ah-meen b'emoonahsh' laimah."
(I have full belief in God.)

   To begin, let me go back six years to March of 1967.
It was then that I fell in love. I was a young girl and
thought my overwhelming love would pass. It did not.

   As you read this letter, I will be getting married to
a man who is much older than I am and, most signifi-
cantly, he is not Jewish. Of course, he will go through
some type of conversion, but I am sure it will not be
according to your rabbinic standard of the Talmud.

   After many, many years of pondering the matter,
which I know in every sense is very wrong, we decided
to marry. I am writing this letter to you because I know
I will not be welcome or accepted in our family again.
Whether your reaction to this is sadness, frustration,
hurt or anger, I do not know. I do know it hurts me
badly to do this to you and to cause you this great shame.

   This "test" was put before me and I did not pass it,
as I thought I would over these years. I have confided in
no one and have written to Candice only.

   How I will miss everyone! I have much to say
and have written and rewritten many long letters. I
thought it best to keep it short. I wanted so much to
bring my husband back home with me.

   Dad and Mom—you have both been wonderful
parents to me. You have given me much and I lacked
nothing. My heart is sad, and I cry bitter tears.

                                        A loving daughter,
                                        Laya

Dear Candice,

I have much to say but will make it short. I've written the details to Mom and Dad and suggest you call them quickly. I am sure you will.

As you read this letter, I will have left home to be married. I met John six years ago and the time has finally come. What I am about to do now is all wrong. It goes against my teaching and everything I believe.

Because I will not be accepted in our family, we will not, to my sadness, see each other again. I will miss your children, whom I have loved so very dearly. There is much to say, though words at a time such as this will be meaningless.

Please kiss the children for me, as I wish I could myself. I wish you many, many years of happiness and joy.

Laya

John's body was firm, his smooth skin warm to the touch. He was handsomely tanned, unlike the pale yeshiva boys I was expected to marry and had dated for the past six years. I caressed the body of my husband and locked my hand in his. We spent that night in a state of endless bliss, high above the twinkling lights of Reno. To feel another human so close, to breathe in his exquisite beauty and tenderness—it was beyond anything I had ever imagined.

We were intermingled, physically and spiritually.

How handsome he was, how full of vigor. My eyes absorbed every inch of his uncovered body.

Even now, I heard a voice that was hard to stifle. *You shall not intermarry with them; you shall not give your daughters to their sons...* I knew these verses of Deuteronomy by heart. Reclining beside this gentile, I knew I was committing a great sin. In the eyes of the community, I had renounced my people.

Like Chava from *Fiddler on the Roof,* I had gone too far by marrying outside the faith. Chava's father Tevya had tolerated one deviation from tradition after another before Chava's sin of marrying a non-Jew had pushed him over the edge. He cried out, "If I try and bend that far, I will break."

But also like Chava and Fyedka, John and I were unable to go on without being together. We were ready to break out in dance and song at the slightest provocation, sure that the audience would weep and root for us—for love!

John sighed. "You're thinking of your family. I can see it in your eyes."

I closed my eyes and shut out the voice. "Not tonight," I said. "Tonight, it's just us."

I felt a fresh warmth radiate across my chest. "I never want this to end," I told him. Now that I had experienced this feeling of freedom and strength, I vowed to never let it go.

"It won't," he answered, pulling me close, our bodies finally joined the way our minds and souls had been for the last six years.

We gazed into each other's eyes, and everything beyond the confines of our bodies ceased to exist.

Three thousand miles away, Morton and Sheila Steinberg were shaken, scared, and overwhelmed. After receiving the mysterious telegram that I had sent from Chicago, they sat up all night, bewildered, unable to construct a single conceivable explanation.

Weeks later, I heard the full account of this night from Candice. She told me that when my follow-up letter arrived from Reno the next day, their confusion turned to stunned horror. They phoned Candice in a state of utter disbelief, just as I knew they would.

"Candice…" my father began.

She wept into the phone, unable to speak, confirming their worst fears.

My mother also began weeping. Their stable universe had turned upside-down.

Candice quickly realized she had to pull herself together. Despite her grief, she somehow rushed to their house from her nearby home, trying to remain calm in the face of her own unraveling.

But by the time she arrived, the humans she called Mom and Dad had dissolved into crumbling vessels of raw emotion. Mother had collapsed sobbing next to the kitchen phone, immobilized by the weight of her imploding world.

Between heaves, she cried, "Why? What did we do? We should have talked to her! We didn't show her enough love! We weren't good parents. Oh, Laya. Laya, I'm so sorry!"

My father, on the other hand, had quickly moved from disbelief to full-on wrath. He strode the living room, his furious pacing providing steady percussion to his operatic calls for vengeance. His rich voice boomed in anger. "I knew that bastard was up to no good. He stole our daughter! We will get her back at any cost. No stone is too heavy to overturn."

Then he turned to my anguished sister. "How could Laya marry a Gentile? Didn't you see it coming?"

Candice had already blamed herself, just like every other member of my family eventually would. The added layers of guilt and shame consumed her.

After the initial round of emotion was spent, my father reverted to his controlled, autocratic self. "She was definitely coerced," my father proclaimed with the certainty of a man used to getting his way.

The two weeping women agreed. It was the only logical explanation.

And thus, the manhunt was set in motion.

CHAPTER 21

Back in Reno, I awoke a married woman. Before this morning, every single sunrise had dragged me from my dreams into the reality of Laya Steinberg, the sheltered heiress of a revered Orthodox dynasty, the daughter no one worried about. I had woken up under my father's ceiling, gotten out of bed, dressed modestly, and walked the well-worn path of my future.

This fresh morning, I awoke on a planet populated only by a husband and wife in a Reno hotel room. This was the world of Laya Martinez. I squeezed John's hand, my husband's hand. Nothing had ever been mine before. Suddenly, everything was.

I had meticulously prepared for this day. I had bought several outfits that I hid in a suitcase in my office. Clothing like this would allow me to feel free, comfortable, and invigorated. Here, there were no laws about covering forbidden skin, no rules about length and color and cut, and no guilt.

I, Laya Martinez, put on a white turtleneck and black slacks. Slacks!

It was unheard of. Insane. Madness.

Bliss.

John beamed at me, as transformed by our union as I was. His normal military stoicism didn't stand a chance against his joy that morning. We practically danced down the hallway, into the elevator, and glided into the hotel restaurant, where we settled in for our first lazy breakfast under the hotel's massive crystal chandelier.

We held hands openly, casually, and freely. The current of love that usually flowed between us had doubled—tripled! —quadrupled!—in size. Now that we had replaced fear with freedom, now that we could show the world how we felt, we did so with abandon. We were married, and no one could take that away from us.

Comfort was a new concept for me. When I managed to pry my eyes away from my magnificent husband, I looked around the dining room in pity at the other couples eating indifferently. None of them seemed to notice how completely in love we were, how perfect the day—the world! After six years of excruciating denial, we no longer had to hide the only emotion that ever really mattered: love.

Almost as amazing as the fact that we were together, or that I was wearing pants, was that we were in a non-kosher restaurant. The waiter brought my egg, toast, and coffee as if it were the most natural, normal thing in the world.

Food had never tasted so good.

I thought, *my hand laid on my husband's chest all through the night. This is my body and my spirit. Happiness is real, and it's mine to take.* I smiled across the table at John and held out my hand to him. For years, he had been telling me how much I was missing. Now, he could witness me discovering the world.

I'm free.

I'm free!

It was an indelible feeling of total freedom.

While I reveled in my newfound independence, across the country my father assembled a crack investigation team.

First, he contacted a private investigator in Reno, where the letters had been postmarked. "My daughter has been lured away by a man. They just married in Reno. I must find out where she is. We must find out what's happening and how to get her back." He gave the investigator all the relevant information. "Please get started immediately. Cost is not an issue. There is no time to waste."

The investigator headed straight to the Reno Justice of the Peace.

My father hired another investigator in New York. "We need to know everything about a man named John Martinez. Find out where he lives and what he was doing before he stole our daughter. Locate, but do not contact, his main associates and any immediate family members. I want to know all of his business, personal and professional. We need to talk to everyone he knows. We need to find out who he is, what he's up to, what his weaknesses are, and what we need to do to get Laya back." My father was used to being the boss. Not only of his own business but of his family. He was desperately trying to be in charge once again.

As soon as the professionals were set in motion, he and my mother packed their bags and boarded the next plane to Reno. "We're the only ones she will listen to," my father said. My mother, still distressed and tearful, agreed.

They were convinced that I had been coerced and something terrible was at play.

As my parents flew west, John and I stood in line to check out of the hotel. I knew we were not going back to New York, but

I had no idea what was next. John had planned a honeymoon, and he outlined the itinerary while we waited. "We're going to drive from Reno to San Francisco, then fly to Miami."

For the first time, I surrendered my responsibilities and put everything in John's hands. I knew nothing about honeymoons. Orthodox couples are separated after their wedding night because the woman is considered impure after bleeding from the puncture of her hymen. Since they are not allowed to touch each other for at least seven days after, a honeymoon would be pointless.

We rented a convertible, loaded our bags, and headed toward the bay. It was my first luxury convertible, my first road trip and my first exposure to the intense beauty of the desert. Dusty brown gave way to lush green as we climbed the peaks of the majestic Sierra Nevada. California's crisp mountain air whipped through my hair, which was finally liberated from its matronly bun. I experienced the landscape with the wonder of a child. Everything was new to me. Everything felt magical.

We never stopped holding hands.

"I can't believe we escaped," I said, throwing my head back to take in the expansive sky.

But we hadn't escaped. Unbeknownst to us, my father's private investigator was watching our every move.

It was easy for him to find us. At the courthouse, he had looked up our marriage record and found the address of the Shapiros, a kind Jewish couple John had been staying with in Reno in order to establish Nevada residency. The Shapiros naively told him what hotel we were staying in, not aware that we were in danger.

He arrived at the hotel while we were checking out and overheard our honeymoon conversation. As soon as we left, he booked my parents a room, filled out a full report, and left it with the front desk. Then he rushed to the car rental agency, arriving there just as we were loading our suitcases into the trunk.

My father only hired the best.

By the time my parents arrived in Reno, it was too late for them to continue the chase: their plane landed late Friday afternoon, with the Sabbath looming at sundown. Perhaps they were fortunate; since they had to rush to the hotel, maybe they hadn't had time to take in all the spectacle that had so excited and repelled me when I had touched down just twenty-four hours before. They were lucky to get to the hotel in time. Searching for us after the sun had set would require them to break all sorts of Sabbath prohibitions: no riding in cars, no writing or telephoning, no spending money. They were forbidden to even push the buttons on the hotel's elevators, as that would be considered "work." They were trapped.

But they had come prepared. They had instructed the investigator to reserve them a room with a refrigerator and kitchenette, so they could prepare the kosher meals they had brought with them. There was no synagogue for my parents to attend, so at sundown, alone, they lit the candles they had brought for the Sabbath. Aside from praying and sleeping, they paced the room from Friday night to sundown on Saturday, silently reading and re-reading the investigator's report and waiting for the opportunity to act.

Meanwhile, I watched the Sabbath sunset in San Francisco.

I thought of the *Shabbos* dinners at my parents' house. Normally I enjoyed the guaranteed pause in everyday worries that came with the holy day, but today I was relieved to be free of the mandatory rituals and outside the realm of my father's authority. Now, I had John to give me that feeling of peace. He was all I needed.

Because I had every intention of continuing to live a religious life, I had packed the items for the proper observance of the holy day in my suitcase alongside my new clothes and accessories: a very small bottle of kosher wine, a set of two candleholders, and two small *challahs*.

But none of it made any sense. I had just committed the most egregious of all sins and now I was blessing the Sabbath. Shame flowed through me for daring to perform this act, and yet, I couldn't stop myself.

It felt foolish.

It felt necessary.

In truth, this was not the first involuntary act I had performed since my marriage. Orthodox Jews make a blessing on every single action, every moment of every day. Would you leave the house without brushing your hair, your teeth? Would you put your car in reverse without looking behind you before you pressed on the pedal? It's the same methodical, conditioned behavior.

John was eager to understand everything about me and my way of life. He admired my character and where I came from. Although he was agnostic, he was raised as a religious Catholic. What he had experienced in the church had no correlation to what he saw in me. Perhaps he thought that my modesty, the gentleness of my manner, and my genuine innocence was a result of my religion. He was interested in learning about Judaism. He wanted to know more. He wanted to know me.

"Laya, why are you putting a kerchief on your head?"

I had no answer.

"Laya, what is the wine for? I'd like to understand what you're doing."

I ignored him and felt terrible for it.

"Laya…"

"I'm just doing what I have to do. I would rather not talk about it." I felt miserable and self-conscious. I realized that what I was doing was ridiculous, yet I couldn't stop myself.

A married woman had to cover her hair, and so I put a kerchief on my head and lit the two candles to welcome the Sabbath. After the hymns, I recited the *Kiddush* (blessing on the wine) and said my prayers because it was Friday night. Like closing one's eyes in order to sleep, who could question such a thing?

I felt very strange. Out of control. Out of my body. Even momentarily out of my mind. In truth, I *was* out of control. This was my brainwashing, and it would take decades to understand how fundamental the constant rituals are in controlling a person's mind. Much, much later, I would free my mind the way I had freed my body. But at the time, I understood none of that. I only knew that I had to perform as I had been programmed to perform since birth.

After the candles were lit and the wine and bread blessed, I took off the kerchief.

I had to stop this charade. I was Jewish and would always be so, regardless of whom I married, no matter what words I uttered, no matter who could see my hair. My children would be Jewish, as Judaism was passed through the maternal line. This was enough.

The rituals, the constant praying, the laws upon laws and rules upon rules—that was all over. The pain and the guilt I felt was for my mother, for the embarrassment she would face in the community. It wasn't religious guilt. I knew who I was and who I would always be.

I folded the kerchief, poured out the wine, and put the bread away.

CHAPTER 22

"THERE ARE THREE STARS IN THE SKY. *SHABBOS* IS over," my mother announced the instant darkness descended Saturday night. "Let's go."

They raced out of the hotel.

Surprised, but not unhappy, Mrs. Shapiro welcomed them. Even in the *shtetls* of New York, Jewish people instinctively opened their homes and put on a *kugel* (a Jewish pasta casserole) when fellow members of the tribe appeared. In Reno, the peculiarity of the arrival of other Jews even called for Mrs. Shapiro's prize *rugelach*, a traditional Jewish cookie that she preserved in the freezer.

In the Shapiro's living room, my father explained their mission. "The man who rented a room from you coerced our daughter into marrying him. He stole our daughter from us! You can understand, he is not Jewish. Besides, he is old enough to be her father. Our lives will never be the same without her. We need her back. He is no good."

The Shapiros were deeply moved by my visibly upset parents, but they had no desire to take sides. They sympathized with the pain my parents were experiencing, but they really had liked John. Everyone liked John.

"We were so fond of him!" Mr. Shapiro proclaimed.

"We knew that his new bride was young and innocent, but we assure you, he always spoke of her with the greatest respect and gentleness," Mrs. Shapiro said.

My parents saw there was no more they would learn in Reno. They flew home and prayed that I would return to New York. They were unsure of their own plans but became even more determined to change mine.

San Francisco's iconic streets reflected my emotions. As we careened around the hairpin turns of Lombard Street, I screamed in terror and delight. The hood of the convertible tipped over steep Filbert Street, and I felt as if we would fall off the edge of the earth. I was in a thrilling new world, surrounded by flowers and safe next to John.

After our magical time in San Francisco, we left for Miami. I watched the waves wash over the sand from the window of the plane as we descended over the city, already knowing I would find peace in this tropical paradise. Before hitting the famed Miami beaches, I needed to buy a swimsuit. We went into a small boutique next to our hotel.

Suddenly, discomfort seized me. Of course, I had owned bathing suits before. I loved to swim. When I was very young, before the tyranny of black hats, wigs, *tzitzits*, and long skirts had descended upon my family, we had gone on vacations and I played in the water for hours.

What had changed in my family and why?

The memory of one Friday night came back to me. I was at our *Shabbos* table, sitting next to my mother, wearing a short sleeve blouse tucked into my skirt. My father had been eying me ever since we stood for *Kiddush*. He kept staring as he blessed the two *challah* rolls, then through the first courses of the Friday night feast. I felt supremely uncomfortable but didn't know why. What had I done?

He looked at my mother and said, "Laya's sleeves are too short. She can no longer wear short sleeves."

My mother was startled. Even at this time, she wore short sleeves on weekdays. Completely taken aback, she said, "Morton, she's not Bat Mitzvah yet." At twelve, Bat Mitzvah age, girls must adhere to the 613 commandments in the bible, but not before.

Nevertheless, from that night on, I wore longer sleeves.

The confusion and shame of that moment still smoldered inside me. What had he seen across that Sabbath table? What had I done wrong? What was there about me, peeking out for my righteous father to see that I could not even see myself? I had always believed I was good, pure, and blameless. How could I fix what I didn't understand?

That small moment of childhood had seared itself into my subconscious.

"Try some on," John urged, pulling me back into the present. He perused the racks. "How about this one?" He held up a yellow two-piece bathing suit.

I was paralyzed, overcome with decades-old shame. "I can't," I said. But as soon as the words passed my lips, I knew they weren't true. Not anymore.

I reached around him and selected a white two-piece with gold accents. "Yellow isn't my color."

Those long, lazy days on the beach were heaven. It had been years since my skin had been exposed to the outside world. But now I reclined on the hotel beach towel with my eyes closed, wearing my new bathing suit, luxuriating in the sensation of sun on skin.

So many of the everyday pleasures I had been denied were opening before me like flowers in an infinite garden. At twenty-five, I had never listened to music outside of synagogue and never watched TV. The only thing better than the beach was the hotel room where there was a television I could watch from my bed. I sat, transfixed, covering my mouth as I laughed at old jokes, which were all new to me. I was drawn into the emotion of every scene.

"If this is how you react to *Mary Tyler Moore*, we have to see a movie," John insisted. "A real, grown-up, modern one."

In a dark movie theater behind our hotel, we watched *The Sting*. I experienced the screen's reality as if it was my own. As soon as the movie ended, I turned to John and said, "Can we stay to see it again?"

Of course, we could. We could do whatever we wished. I could even eat all the ice cream I wanted. As John and I strolled past an ice-cream parlor, there was nothing to stop us from going inside.

"I would like a small vanilla cone, please," I said. "No, a small vanilla cone with sprinkles. No, a strawberry sundae, please."

The woman waited to see if I would change my mind again. John waited, too.

"No," I said. "I would like a banana split with extra hot fudge sauce."

When the private investigator found John's mother, my mother and father were elated. Finally, they could talk to a fellow parent. Surely, she would understand their plight. They phoned Della Martinez at her home in the Pennsylvania coal country.

Of course, she knew me, she told them. "I've met her twice. Loved her."

She didn't know about the marriage, but she wasn't surprised. "I rooted for my son as he struggled through his first marriage for the sake of his kids. But it was never really a marriage."

My parents were mortified. The woman was clearly crazy.

"Laya is twenty-five, but given her sheltered life, she is equivalent to a seventeen-year-old," my father implored. "She is innocent and does not know the world. Your son is old enough to be her father."

Of course, my father did not care about John's age. He was eleven years older than my mother. He was only trying to grasp an argument that might sway her. Della Martinez had enough. She was no fool; she understood what my parents were not-so-subtly trying to say.

"I raised a man of honor," she told them. "John is forty-three, but young at heart like a twenty-two-year-old."

My father cracked. "She is a Jewish girl, forbidden to marry a Gentile."

But Della held her ground, and my father hung up in frustration.

Deep down, Della was a religious woman, and she had sympathy for my parents. But she also had sympathy for her son, which they could never understand.

In Miami, John suggested we do something that would expand my horizons even further. "Let's go to a burlesque show," he said. I had been to a few talents shows in high school, but he assured me this was something different. We sat right in the front.

This was no high school talent show.

I have always been a very modest person. Not for religious reasons, it's just the way I prefer to carry myself. Immodesty, however, is the theme of burlesque shows. The songs, the dances, the outfits, the...insinuations. *Am I really sitting here?* I thought to myself, overwhelmed. *This is contemptible, forbidden!* But I also found it enticing, so daring, so exciting, so...

I couldn't express what I was feeling. I was terrified at something I still can't explain. I was embarrassed for the dancers, for me. If anyone from home had seen me there, I would have died on the spot and been grateful for the mercy. I worried about what people thought when they saw us together. I tried to hide behind John so no one would come over and say, "How old are you, little girl? Is this the first time your Dad is taking you to see a show like this?"

But I soon realized that no one there cared about me. Everyone was there to see the show. And when I let myself relax and watch the acts, it became thrilling. All these private, secret things were embraced in the open. Everybody was enjoying themselves, reveling in the taboo of it. Not exactly my cup of tea, but such an exciting brew to taste.

The next night, John took me to a drag show. It was exhilarating, funnier, and cleaner than the burlesque. As I watched the men cavort on stage as women, I recalled a passage in Deuteronomy 22.5: *The woman shall not wear that which pertains unto a man, neither shall a man put on a woman's garment for all who do so are an abomination unto the Lord your God.* That passage always confused me. Why would a man want to dress like a woman? Women dress so much less comfortably. I still didn't understand why *these* men did, but I didn't care. They were having fun. I was having fun. That was what mattered.

I realized something important that night. My life, with all its rules and sacrifices, was supposed to draw me closer to the sacred. Orthodox Judaism claims that the surest path to the sacred is through personal experience. But I never really felt much of anything. Yet this—my honeymoon, my husband, our whole world—*this* was sacred. I had finally started to experience the full range of emotions: pure love, pure joy, pure trust, and pure fear. And with John, I finally experienced pure freedom.

I would never again wake up as Laya Steinberg in my parents' house, leading a double life and doing things I didn't want to do.

I was free to live.

The investigator tailed us all the way from Reno. He knew about our car rental before we drove down Lombard Street. He watched me sunbathe in the two-piece bathing suit from afar so he could inform my parents of my sin. He watched me eat a banana split and walk blinking out of a darkened movie theater. He sat tables away at the burlesque and drag shows, watching me let go and have fun. He recorded it all in his notebooks and in photos, all of which were sent to my parents.

I had no idea he was watching our every move at the time, and obviously, I'm glad I didn't. Those memories will always be tainted with the knowledge that all through those first free days, my family was still watching me, still prying and judging, violating my most fundamental right: that my life is my own.

At the time, it was painful thinking about what my family was going through because of my betrayal. I loved them, and if there were any way I could have had John and them, I would have. This was an unbearable situation. I had the rest of my life to process my painful decision. I assumed they would write me off, never to speak to me again.

But I was about to learn that they did not plan on letting me go. They were going to fight with everything they had to get me back. When we returned to New York, the honeymoon was over, in more ways than one.

Two letters were waiting for me at the office:

For blessed be His Name

Dear Laya, to live,

Your pathetic letters stabbed us—and our hearts went out for you. How you suffered with your burden! You are still our daughter and will always be. I want to talk to you.

We did not want to break away from you. Even though you sinned, you are still a Jew.

For everyone's sake, please call me and let me know when I can meet with you. We left N.Y. for Reno on the next plane after we received your letter. We are staying in Reno for Shabbos because we couldn't get home in time for Saturday. There is nothing here, but many people get caught in places for Shabbos and make the best of it.

Please call Candice or me — we can understand this problem. I have confidence in you that all of the other commandments you are keeping are with exactness. If one does a single sin, you should be 1,000 times more diligent in all of the other commandments.

Remember you are our daughter and we want you to always be. I'm waiting...

Mom

P.S. No one knows anything yet.

Dearest Laya,

There are no words to express my heartbreak at the thought of never seeing you again!

You're still my sister! I love you dearly. Why can't I see you again?

You say there is "much to say." Why can't we speak to each other? I grieve to think that you don't want to see me again or to even talk to me again. I'm your sister, through thick or thin.

Please, please, call at the first chance you have.

Candice

Upon returning from Reno, my mother walked into the bank, just as she usually did three or four times a week.

"Hello, Mrs. Steinberg, how are you today?" The bank officer pulled back a chair, so she could sit at his desk. They continued with small talk about their families.

"I need a withdrawal slip," she said nonchalantly. "I'll be making a withdrawal from my daughter's account."

"Certainly! Just sign here and take it to the teller."

And just like that, my mother emptied my bank account. It wasn't hard in those days, when small-town bankers knew their customers personally. The employees trusted my mother, an important client for decades.

I didn't blame the bank.

Nor did I blame my mother. I had done great damage to her and believed she deserved everything I owned. If I could have given her more, I would have. For her part, she believed that by taking my money, I would be forced to return back to her.

It wasn't about the money. She was doing God's work.

CHAPTER 23

As our plane touched down in New York, the solemn reality of our situation hit me full force. I could no longer sit across the kitchen table from my mother and talk about fashion in *The New York Times*, the daily happenings at home, or my nieces and nephews.

In Florida, it all felt far away. Now, back home in New York, I realized I didn't know what home meant anymore. I had thought that now, married to John, I was free. But in truth, the battle had just begun.

John and I walked off the tarmac together, gathered our luggage, and found my Pinto in the freezing parking lot. John took the driver's seat. "We'll go directly to the office." We had a pull-out sofa there to sleep on.

Despite the situation, I felt calm as we leisurely drove through the dark streets of Long Island. We arrived at the office around 10 pm, so the place was mercifully deserted. Once upstairs, we quickly got ready for bed, opened the pull-out sofa, and slipped under the covers.

We smiled at each other. Night number one—of the rest of our lives.

The following morning, we awoke early and were out the door before the other tenants arrived. After a quick breakfast at the coffee shop, I headed to the bank and discovered my emptied accounts. "It's okay. I still have cash," I told John when I returned.

I was an earner and a saver all my life, and never put all my money in one place. John, on the other hand, had nothing. He had willingly handed over everything: his house, his car, and his accounts in the divorce. He felt that his ex-wife and children needed the funds more than we did. I was glad that he took care of her and the children, confident that we would build an empire of our own.

We had a small business account, but we needed that for growing our client base. John needed to kick the company into high gear—fast. I had income from the print shop, but not enough for what we needed.

We were facing financial hardship and uncertainty that we hadn't anticipated, but we didn't care. We had each other and that was all that mattered. We knew we could make it work.

We rented an apartment near our offices using almost all the cash we had left. It took time, but gradually we earned enough money and got everything in the apartment exactly the way we wanted.

It's so easy to do anything when you're happy and in love. All my thoughts were positive. I worked all day, knowing that whatever happened, I would go home and see the person I loved. I lived for those moments with John. Just to be together, even if not a word passed between us.

In our apartment building, I discovered a world I never knew existed, and each revelation was more amazing than the last. My new next-door neighbor, a lovely woman with a six-year-old girl, had a husband who often stayed out late. She confided in me that he wasn't at the office, but at Alcoholics Anonymous meetings.

I had never known such a thing existed—good, responsible, family people who were alcoholics. In my simplistic childhood world, alcoholics were bums on the street.

One night when I was reading a book in bed with John beside me, I asked him, "What's this word? War?"

"You know what war is," he said, incredulous.

I pointed at the word I didn't know in the book and he burst out laughing.

"It's not said like that. It's pronounced *hoor*. It's a prostitute. You know what that is, it's in the bible."

Of course, I knew what a prostitute was. I just had no idea they existed in the modern world. My idea of a prostitute was Rahab, best known for helping Joshua's spies escape from Jericho after they had sneaked into the city in the book of Joshua.

I still had so much to learn.

As a child, Saturdays had always been my favorite days. Now, they were even better.

John and I would wake up leisurely, no rush, just the two of us and the joy of life.

When we had finally pulled ourselves out of bed, I would set the table and John would make a simple, delicious breakfast with eggs that tasted like nothing I had ever eaten before. Even the bread was toasted and buttered to unique perfection. After so many years of thinking that I didn't like food, I now realized that I just hadn't been able to enjoy anything involving sensual pleasure.

There were so many years to make up for. I got up from the table every ten minutes to put my arms around John's neck and gently kissed him on the cheek.

We sat together, ate, and talked about the week.

I remained a Sabbath observer, so I would not ride in a car. John would go to his gun club, where he was president, and shoot skeet or trap. I would stay home and make sure our apartment was spotless. I couldn't wait until John returned so we could finish our Saturday routine. He would make a simple dinner while I set a formal table in the dining room.

We would eat, enjoying every bite and looking forward to what was to come. John would cap it off by making each of us a grand ice cream sundae with crushed nuts, chocolate sauce, and whipped cream.

Afterward, we'd sit on the sofa and watch our favorite shows on TV. Every show was only thirty minutes long. Never enough! *All in the Family*, followed by *The Jeffersons*, then *The Mary Tyler Moore Show*, *The Bob Newhart Show*, *The Carol Burnett Show*, the *Dick Cavett Show*, and finally, *Saturday Night at the Movies*.

It was all so new to me. I soaked up every joke, every set, and every nuance of emotion.

I was in a state of complete happiness. John and I were so in sync that when I looked at my reflection in the mirror, I saw John's face staring back at me. He was my soulmate.

I later learned this feeling of utter tranquility was called *ataraxia*, or a complete mental calmness. Ataraxia, combined with freedom from fear and freedom from physical pain, was happiness in its highest form as described by the philosopher Epicurus.

He was right on target.

Such perfection of mental state cost us no more than the price of a quart of ice cream and some toppings.

We were free and in love. We were alone in the world, but we would make it work.

But we weren't alone. The private detective my parents had hired watched and documented every step of our new lives.

Not long after we were settled, my family ambushed me with the one weapon I was still defenseless against; my beloved mother.

CHAPTER 24

I WALKED UP TO MY PRINT SHOP, AN OLD BRICK STOREFRONT overlooking the main road. I was eager to start up the presses and get to work, but I couldn't get rid of the knot in my stomach.

Two days earlier, I had gotten a letter from my mother. She had scribbled in Hebrew over the letter I had sent her from Reno, essentially declaring that I was dead to the family. That wasn't surprising. I knew I would be discarded.

It was the cruelty of her expression that had stunned me, and I was aghast at the meanness of her words. My mother had never been harsh and unfeeling. I tried to brush it off, but clearly, her heartless letter had disturbed me on a deeper level than I had admitted to myself.

Determined to have a productive day, I opened the door to the shop.

A tall man dressed all in black waited inside.

It was my Uncle Nathan, my father's youngest brother, who had come from Israel. He had a broad frame and stood six feet tall. He flashed the wide, warm smile of an old friend meeting me by lucky coincidence instead of the grimace of a man who had just flown halfway around the world to rescue his niece from hellfire.

Behind him stood my mother.

She wore a simple, modest, blue pin-stripe dress. Her lipstick was neatly applied. To my employees, I'm sure she appeared proper and poised, her chin held high with determination. But behind this mask, her face was gaunt and her eyes were red from recently shed tears. She stared at me as if she was seeing my ghost across an unfathomable chasm and was prepared to fight until she got what she had come for.

I was too stunned to speak. I wanted to go to her, to comfort her.

My uncle, always good-natured and boisterously friendly, began to introduce himself and my mother to my bookkeeper and the other employees who were emerging from the press and processing rooms to get a peek at this odd pair.

I couldn't let my family humiliate me in front of my employees. I had to take control of the situation—fast.

"Let's go outside." I ushered them out the door.

The three of us stood awkwardly on the sidewalk. I didn't offer my uncle a hug because aside from parents and spouses, men and women did not touch each other, even relatives. With my heart pounding, I hugged my mother stiffly. The familiar smell of her perfume almost brought me to tears. *Who bought you flowers last Sabbath since I couldn't? Who will brush your hair and help you get dressed up for special events? Who asks you about your day and then listens to your replies?* I couldn't ask her these questions, but I didn't have to. I already knew the answers.

Every Friday, for the last three years, I brought her a bouquet of flowers for the Sabbath. I also taught her how to put on makeup and do her hair before every social event. These times together were special.

Next to my huge, grinning uncle, she looked frail and supremely unhappy. She was torturing herself with thoughts of what she couldn't have, suffering pain in her body and her soul. I could carry on because of my happiness; she had shut down from her sadness.

Wasn't there some way to talk as mother and daughter? But the wall between us was too high, stones placed by centuries of tradition and unforgiving dogma.

My uncle smiled a huge, warm smile. "How are you? Let's go somewhere and talk. Tell me how you're doing. I want you to find happiness, and I want to help you with your life." He was a leader in the Jewish world, idolized by millions for his work with "lost Jews," people who wanted to return to their Judaic roots after lifetimes spent astray.

I was growing desperate in the face of my miserable mother, crumbling inside my own stone-faced facade. "Let's not talk here. How about later tonight?"

"Sure, no problem." He nodded to my mother. "We'll have coffee later and then we can talk."

Uncle Nathan was calm and confident, but my mother's grief was too raw to allow for this delay. He began to walk away, but she was riveted to the pavement. Unable to touch her, my uncle wasn't sure what to do. Still refined and proper, head held high, she was resolute. My mother, who always did what she was told, was now being told to leave her daughter here in this unholy place with these unholy people and she was not about to do so.

Uncle Nathan leaned down and whispered something into her ear, but she stood her ground.

I stood mine.

I don't remember how he finally got my mother into the car. As they drove away, my heart broke.

Uncle Nathan came back six hours later, alone. As I listened to him speak, I couldn't erase the image of my mother, so unhappy, so broken. I had to give her something to hope for, something to soften this sudden violent separation. She was imprisoned by her dogmatic religion, but I still loved her. She was still my mother. This was the child inside me, but it was also the human inside me. I was not a robot, able to cut off emotion in pursuit of pure rationality.

"Come home this Sunday. We'll discuss the situation there," my uncle said soothingly.

I thought of my old schoolmate Sarah, locked in her parents' home. Surely that couldn't happen to me, an adult woman with a husband and a business. Could it?

"We can solve this situation," my uncle pleaded. "Bring John. We'll all talk."

The "situation" had only two solutions: I leave John or continue in this way, shaming my family and ending up in eternal damnation.

With the terrible image of my mother in my head, I thought about the possibility of John converting. It made no sense to think that John could convert in a way that my family would accept. It was one thing to become a Reform Jew, but to learn and live the way of an Orthodox man was nearly impossible. But what if he did? Maybe he would meet my beautiful family and think it was worth it.

He admired my parents, and my entire family. He appreciated how well they had raised me, and he respected what they had been through and what they had achieved. Maybe, I thought, he would be able to live as an Orthodox man, they will welcome him, and we'll all be able to sit together around the Sabbath table just as I had dreamed.

In my heart of hearts, I knew it couldn't be. Even if John did convert, they would never accept his conversion as good enough. But for my mother's sake, I had to try something.

I agreed we would go to my parents' house the following Sunday.

The instant Uncle Nathan was gone, I regretted my decision and began to waiver. John would never be accepted, and we *all* knew it.

But they seemed to have anticipated this. Two days later, a letter arrived from my mother that was kind and loving. With it, she included a letter from my younger brother, Asher. For years, Asher and I were the only two children remaining in the house after the others had married or, in Mordechai's case, left for boarding school.

The two of us shared a special relationship, especially when my parents were not at home. We walked together for hours, he confided all of his fears and could tell me anything, knowing full well they were safe with me.

He had a thick head of hair and I used to brush it with mousse to thicken the look. As I styled it this way and that, he watched excitedly in the mirror, laughing, and joking about the different hairstyles. We loved to spend time together, especially when we were free of my parents' watchful eyes. My little brother never got this kind of attention from anyone else.

Asher was sent off to boarding school just months before I left for Reno, so I had assumed my leaving would be less painful for him.

When I read his letter, I realized how deeply my departure had hurt him. I was his closest sibling and the only one he related to in the family.

> *Dear Laya,*
>
> *What is happening? To me, it's like a dream. (I'm sure you understand.) Well, this is no time to go through all the junk! What should I tell you? You know me, and I know you! Please call!! I don't have to tell you who I am, and I can comprehend stuff about anything, and you know it. After all, you are my sister and give me one call — even if it should be the last one!!!*
>
> *Your Brother (forever),*
> *Asher*

He later told me, "You abandoned me." He was right, and I never forgave myself for distancing myself from him. At the time, we were so close I was afraid he might have chosen to follow me. I couldn't let my mother lose another child.

For my suffering mother, for my childish hope, and for my dear brother, I would go home and hear them out.

CHAPTER 25

CAREFUL NOT TO HOLD HANDS OR EVEN TOUCH ACCIDEN-
tally John and I walked together up the slate pathway and
climbed the steps to the front door. I was dressed according to
the strict codes of my childhood. Anyone watching from the
street would have thought I had never left home.

My mother met us at the door.

"Hello, Mr. Martinez," my mother welcomed John politely.
First names were out of the question.

"Hello," John responded courteously.

It felt like a dream to be home with John. Was this really
happening?

Mother led us to the center hall. To the right was the dining
room, with walls covered in hand-painted murals and the huge
table that evoked so many memories.

Maybe nothing has really changed, I told myself, even though
I knew it couldn't be true. But, I had never expected to be in this
house again and here I was. Maybe I had gotten it all wrong.

Hope and love are powerful emotions.

Everyone had come: my parents, my sister Candice, her
husband, and my two uncles. Everything seemed normal except
for the lack of my nieces and nephews. There were always so
many children laughing and playing around, but not today.

This was not a situation suitable for children, and that
made my anxiety return in full force. "Mr. Martinez, welcome

to my home." In an instant, my father and his gang of brothers had separated us and were steering John away from me into the dining room. "Have a seat and some pastries that my wife made." I had wished that John could sit beside me at the family holiday table, and now here he was at that table, with my family.

"Laya, let's sit in the living room," Candice said, pulling me away from the men. She led me to the seafoam green couch upon which I had endured so many uncomfortable lectures from my father for so many years.

Why had I come? What were they saying to John? What would they say to me?

I reminded myself that I was here for my mother. If there was some small hope that we could work something out, for her sake I would endure my discomfort. I loved her and my heart ached for her. But I was starting to understand what I was up against. I knew the ancient man-made laws in the Talmud. You were either in or out. There were no shades of gray. The fear of losing a member of the community to reason was too great to allow for any room to compromise.

Candice rose and left the room, leaving me alone with the roaring fire.

I slid down to the other side of the couch and remembered:

Sitting on this couch with my mother, waiting for my father to come home from the synagogue, thinking he was the messiah, thinking he had all the answers, that he would fly us to Jerusalem on his back. The laughter of my sisters, the smiles of my small brothers, the many guests who came and went, my nephews and nieces, I miss so much.

My Uncle Judah strode into the room. Immediately I was struck by his harsh, relentless manner which was in stark contrast to my Uncle Nathan's genuine kindness. Uncle Judah towered over me, more than six feet tall. He was slimmer than his brother Nathan and had none of his warmth. He was a neat and handsome man and I had loved him until one day, he shamed that love out of me.

I was eleven years old, standing on the stairway when he came through the front door to visit. I was so excited to see him, that I wanted to jump into his arms. I shouted, "Catch me! Catch me!" He looked up at me disapprovingly and said, "You're too old now. A girl your age does not jump to her uncle." I was crushed. I felt confused and embarrassed, forever after uncomfortable in his presence.

Now, feeling ashamed and guilty as I had then, I sat on the couch, making sure my skirt covered my knees.

Uncle Judah pulled over a chair from the card table just as my father had after another one of my failed dates. He sat down, leaned in, and launched his offensive. "We're on this earth for one purpose—to serve God. It is against the Torah to marry a non-Jew. You have sinned."

I hadn't known then that there was actually no such thing written in the Torah.

"You must repent immediately and leave this man, or you will be severely punished in the world to come."

This is the last time I will sit here in humiliation. Be patient. Wait it out. I've done it a million times before. It will be over eventually, and I will be free. I can endure this. I must do it for my mother...

My uncle continued, "Liken this life to a vestibule, a practice for the world to come. Even if you never get married, even if you live a life of suffering, you must repent. This world is not about your happiness. It's about serving God, and you will be happy enough doing just that, knowing you will be forgiven and enter the gates of heaven. You must be humble, serve God and obey his commandments. How dare you disrespect God and your parents. You must suffer and pray for forgiveness!"

I watched the logs in the fire burn and collapse into themselves. On and on he raged, mercilessly assaulting me with the litany of ills I had brought upon the family by my unacceptable choice. Then he conjured the horrors of what was to come. My soul would wander forever and ever, and I would be cursed and destined as the wicked, to *Gehenna*. (Gehinnom) a valley in Jerusalem, where some of the kings of Judah sacrificed their children by fire.

My uncle never took his eyes off of me, never let an instant of silence interrupt his tirade.

Finally, his anger spent, he stalked out of the room.

I hadn't said a single word.

I took a breath and looked around me, grateful for the silence.

Now what?

Uncle Nathan entered. I thought back to years earlier when he proposed to his wife in this very room. Four of us children hid all in a row against the wall with our ears pinned to the wallpaper on the stairway, eavesdropping on them, trying to hear every word. How excited we were! He was sweet and loving to us, always.

"You have to leave John, but *you will be happy*," he said with a comforting smile as he sat down beside me. "We'll find someone *else* for you to love. It will all work out. Life is good, serving God in the right way, but you must take decisive action now."

Nathan's kindness was worse than Judah's wrath.

As he spoke, I realized that each of my uncles honestly believed that I was sinning against God and that I would go to hell. For that, I could forgive them. But I was beginning to sense that these men weren't only thinking of my soul, they were leaders in their communities and had to set examples. My soul was important, but they also had to protect the family image within the community and to the outside world, regardless of my needs.

They said I should only live for God and not for happiness. Meanwhile, they lived as gods, worshiped by the community. That was what brought them their personal happiness.

This was only the briefest stirring of a thought, just beyond my grasp. I was still too under the spell of authority to be able to translate this thought into resentment.

I only wanted to stop hurting my mother. I understood the shame I had brought on her and I wanted it to end. Hell on Earth wasn't being barraged with endless threats. It was seeing for myself how badly I had wounded the mother I dearly loved, and how easy it would be to make it all right.

The afternoon was an endless nightmare.

They were going about this all wrong, with threats and anger. Every dire warning and furious outburst further closed the door my family was trying so hard to pry open.

Meanwhile, John sat at the dining room table in front of a dazzling display of cakes, cookies, and fruit which he enjoyed while they drilled him for details. *Who are you? Where are you from? When and why did you get married the first time? What would you do if someone stole your daughter from you?* On and on, they continued into the late afternoon.

Their guilt trip had no impact on John. He sat, listened, and politely disagreed with their pronouncements and assumptions. They hadn't been able to get under his skin, because again, they had erred in their strategy. Instead of inviting him in, they attacked him. Going into the meeting, he had actually liked and respected my family. But now, watching their condemning faces up close, he finally understood how much they passionately despised him.

He saw their hatred for what it was.

The ordeal eventually ended. Walking to our car, my knees trembled. I could not get into the passenger's seat fast enough. The moment the door closed, I felt safe again sitting next to my husband.

"It was horrible. What did they tell you? What did they ask you? What did you say to them?"

"I told them the truth: that we love each other and that was all that mattered. But more interesting is what I learned."

I held my breath.

"Your parents hired a private investigator to follow us. They found the family I lived with in Nevada who told them all about my apartment in Queens and our offices in Long Island. They even talked to Annie and to my mother." Annie was John's ex-wife.

"They spied on us?"

"I don't blame them," John said.

I was too shocked to respond.

"I can understand your parents. They see a young girl taken away from them by a stranger.

"I can't believe you're taking their side."

"I'm not. I'm just *seeing* their side. It's not the same thing."

"Weren't you even a little bit angry at how they treated you?"

"Yes. When they kept telling me that I was old enough to be your father. That bothered me."

I smiled, and he did too, and I knew then that we were going to be okay.

Or, at least I thought so.

The next day I was back at the print shop, sitting at my desk when the phone rang.

My assistant at the front desk answered. "Oh. Oh—sir, please calm down." She put the receiver to her chest and yelled, "Mrs. Martinez, there's a very upset man on the phone for you."

I picked up the phone and heard a frantic voice on the other end.

"A man... your father... I am so sorry... I know it was wrong... I didn't mean to..."

It took me a moment to realize it was Charlie, the property manager of the building that housed our new computer offices. It took another moment to realize that he had let my father into our empty facility.

Poor Charlie. He was powerless in the face of the rage and righteousness of my father. I knew how he felt. "I'll be right over,"

I called John, breathless. "My father came to the office and Charlie let him in!"

"What? Why?"

"I must get over there right away. Please pick me up now. I'll wait for you outside."

John's car screeched to a stop in front of the print shop, barely stopping long enough for me to hurl myself inside.

"I'm going in to talk to him," he said through gritted teeth. He strangled the wheel in a death grip as he recklessly pulled back into traffic.

I shook my head emphatically. "That's a bad idea."

"This needs to end, Laya."

It took less than two minutes to drive between our offices. I didn't have much time.

"Please *do not* come upstairs to the office. Stay down here in the car, and I will go up to see my father. *DO NOT* come up, regardless of your feelings. No matter what. I want to handle this myself!"

John pulled up in front of our building.

"Promise me you won't come up. It will only end in disaster. I know you both so well."

He shut down the engine. I put a calming hand on his shoulder. He took a deep breath. "Okay. Yes."

I opened the heavy car door. My heart was pounding so hard, I could hear it thumping. When I was on my father's terrain, I could leave. What would I do when he was abusive on my turf? Demand that he leave? Demanding anything of my father was not possible.

Charlie was in the front hall, looking sheepish. "I'm so sorry..."

I felt sorry for him, but I was also furious. Was this how all men were, either dominating or dominated? Was that how the whole world separated into two?

With a heavy heart, I climbed the stairs.

The office door was open. Inside, my father paced the room like a caged tiger. His five-foot-seven-and-three-quarter-inch frame, usually tall and erect, was bent in focused consternation.

Charlie had been doomed: my father always got his way, either by bullying force or charm and persuasion.

I prayed that this time he would try the latter.

I paused before making my presence known, trying to control my trembling. As soon as I pushed the door wider, I saw I had misinterpreted my father's state of mind. This wasn't the dominating, powerful man I knew. He was completely distraught.

He must have seen the same in me.

We stared at each other, two miserable humans, not knowing how to proceed in this uncharted territory.

I gestured for him to sit.

He did.

I gently pulled my chair next to him. "Dad…"

Before I could say another word, John burst into the room. Feeling powerless and utterly betrayed, I jumped up, trying to move between the men. "John. No. Please. You must go downstairs immediately."

Instead, John approached my suffering father.

My father, with immense passion and emotion, reached out to him. His voice shook with dismay. "How can you take my daughter away from me?"

I had never seen my father so distressed, so overwhelmed with grief.

John, seeing this too, froze. He looked from me to my father.

Moments after he sat down next to my father, fear overtook John. He grabbed my father by the lapels, lifted him to his feet and shook him.

My father's eyes grew wide and his strong body went limp with anguish. Blood appeared at the corner of his mouth, as he bit his lip in bewilderment.

I could not comprehend what was happening. Who was this man I loved laying hands on my father? I panicked, bolting out the door and careening down the stairs.

"Laya, wait!" John was stumbling behind me. "I'm sorry. I'm so, so sorry!" John pleaded. "I just... I snapped"

In a daze, I somehow found myself in the passenger seat of our car. John was beside me. "Forgive me. Forgive me, Laya. I didn't mean to touch him! I was afraid you'd change your mind. I saw his face and I thought that maybe you'd go back to him."

My husband had grabbed my father, a man who didn't have the slightest idea how to fight back, who wasn't even looking for a fight in the first place. *Logically, could I understand John's fear?* He knew how much power my father had over me. He saw that my father's distress could break me in a way his anger never could. But physical violence, it was unthinkable. There was nothing more inconceivable.

A huge crash sounded from above. Glass showered everywhere as a hunk of metal exploded onto the asphalt not twenty feet from our car. I learned later that it was our IBM Selectric typewriter that my father had hurled through the window of our second-floor office.

John pressed his foot to the accelerator, and we sped away. The whole way home, I kept replaying my father's bewildered face in my mind, the blood on his mouth, the terror in his trembling voice, and the barrage of glass and metal.

This was all foreign to me. People in my world did not behave this way, with violence and impulse.

I raced into our apartment and called my mother. I described the mad scene that had taken place at the office. "I am so worried about what will happen to Dad."

"See? This is why you should come back. You belong at home."

Who could imagine what the trip back home must have been like for my proud and always-in-charge father?

Now John was truly a demon in their eyes.

And what was I to them? A dupe? A victim? Or a willing participant in the destruction of my own family? I was sure that this time, it was really the end. I would never see or speak to them again.

No matter how I tried, I could not obliterate the horror of that day from my mind.

CHAPTER 26

"I WISH I COULD BE IN A CAR ACCIDENT AND LOSE MY recent past. My parents would pick me up from the hospital, and I wouldn't remember anything beyond the first nineteen years of my life. I could start all over again, not hurting anyone."

These were the despairing thoughts that ran through my head. I fantasized constantly about what would have happened if I had never met John, and never had to choose between him and my family. I didn't regret my marriage, but I deeply felt the bitter pain it caused the people I loved.

Six months of silence...

And then another letter arrived.

Dear Laya,

It's the anniversary of Granddaddy's death, and I am hoping that maybe his soul will intercede for us and bring you back.

It was just Passover (we missed you so much) and I was thinking that maybe God could save us all from our various slaveries. I think about it when we sit in our house, when we walk on the road, when we go to sleep, and when we get up. I think between headaches, during praying, and when I say Psalms every night.

I have been thinking for over five long, sad months: what did we do and how to make amends? How to make you understand how much you mean to us, and how we are praying to fill that void that exists in our family. How can I get you to understand that when one takes something for granted and it disappears, it is missed that much more?

Laya, each day brings us to more understanding of your feelings. I won't be dishonest and say you did right because you know that is not true, and honest with you I have always been. I do say that I can understand you and your feelings. We love you dearly, but you didn't feel it, and we were wrong in not conveying it to you properly.

We had a tense household, we did not give you the communication and thoughtfulness that you needed and deserved. We faltered along the way. We are guilty, we sinned. But we are changing, we are learning to relax, we are learning how to be considerate of each other and to accept each other for ourselves alone and not what we represent. We find the good qualities in each other and do not harp on the faults.

We try to talk together, think together, and enjoy ourselves together. Sure, we've gotten help to try to understand you and your feelings and what you lacked from us. We needed help. We want to fill that void that hurts us, but it is not "us" that is the concern. It is you. We're on the second part of the road; you're on the first. That's our concern. We all miss you desperately, and we all need you. We have so many things to look forward to and share together.

I am sending you a picture that I cherish very much. I have no negative, no copy, but I happily send it to you. I hope that you will cherish it too, and one day we will admire it together. It represents a very happy household. Our arms are linked together in love and admiration. You are a big part of this picture.

Laya, let's bring this picture up to date. I could write more and more and as it says in the scriptures: if the waters were ink, it wouldn't be enough to write in praise of God. We say to a child, "We can't approve of what you did, but you, we love."

Love, Mom

It saddened me that she took the blame upon herself and was suffering so greatly.

John and I were the best-kept secret in all of New York. Although six months had passed since our wedding, only a few people in my parents' community knew about us. My sister Syrle, who lived in Israel, knew nothing. My parents simply hadn't told her. As far as Syrle and her family were concerned, I was still living at home, working at my job, and looking for a husband.

But now, Syrle was coming back to attend a wedding with her eldest daughter, nine-year-old Ella. My parents had no intention of telling her the truth about my situation. But, of course, there was a problem: if I wasn't living at home, where was I? I either had to be at home or be married to a Jewish man. There was no other suitable option.

"Can you come to stay at the house next weekend?" my mother asked. Her phone call came just a few days after her letter had arrived. "Stay here, as if nothing has happened? Syrle doesn't know you've moved away. If you're not at the airport, eagerly waiting to see her, they'll think something is strange."

John thought this was the wildest thing he had heard yet. Still, it was another opportunity to make amends to my mother for all the pain I had caused her. If I could pretend for Syrle, then my mother wouldn't have to bear telling her the truth. And somehow, I knew that she couldn't endure it.

"For one weekend, I can pretend," I told John. "I owe her at least that."

It was absurd, and yet I agreed to act as if I still lived at home, unmarried. Six years of secret romance had never happened, nor had my elopement, the private investigators, the inquisition, and the hurtful letters. After all, I had been pretending for six years before I left, what was one more weekend?

"Take off your wedding rings before you come into the house," my mother said. "We can't have Syrle seeing you wearing a wedding band."

I fully understood my mother's need for this pretense. She was putting on a front for everybody: her community, her synagogue, even her own family. To John's dismay, I took off my wedding rings, hid them in a drawer, and packed my bags for my parents' home.

The two days that followed were like a dream forgotten upon awakening as if my mind was trying to protect me from the pain. I had last seen Syrle ten years ago. Then, I had been her beloved sister. Now, I was a play-actor in this grotesque charade.

"Laya! Look at you!" Syrle stood tall and slim. She was stately, even regal. When Syrle entered a room, her aura of authority caused heads to turn.

Even now in the airport, people were staring. She had such a presence. She was self-assured and unaffected by the interest of the crowd. She looked uniquely powerful. I had so admired her, and upon seeing her now that admiration rushed back to me. She beamed with pride as she presented her nine-year-old child to me for the first time. "Ella, this is your Aunt Laya!"

My stomach churned as I embraced the small girl. I hated this travesty of deceit. If I had blurted out the truth, Syrle would have ripped this child from my arms. She would have refused to come back to the house with us, to stay even one minute in my parents' house if I were present. She would have prayed for me as if I were dead.

Instead, we spent most of the next day preparing meals for the Sabbath. Mother was too quiet as we put the salad together. I went through the motions, feeling like a stranger in the house where I had lived for twenty-five years.

I felt out of place, like one of the many guests we had over the years, looking in. It was like leaving my body, watching my family from afar, no longer a part of them. We all put on the show of being a perfect, happy family like consummate performers. My sister and her daughter were so excited to be there, that they did not seem to notice.

The act was working.

As the sun set, Asher walked with my father to the synagogue for evening services. We women stayed home to pray and to make sure all was ready for when the men returned. At the dinner table, my father led the rituals. He gave a sermon on the Torah laws and told biblical stories to which my niece listened with rapture. In her eyes, I saw the wonder I used to feel when listening to my father speak. *My father, surely the messiah! He will fly me to Israel on his back.* Did all little girls feel that way at one time about their fathers? And then, did those girls grow up and see a more complicated picture?

I watched Syrle watch my father with the same look on her face.

I thought to myself, *there are two worlds: secular and religious.* My father allowed my sisters and their families to exist only in this religious world because of his great generosity. He protected them from the real world. They were grown, with babies, but they would always be children, asking his permission, beholden to him.

What he was doing for them was generous, Godly, and I wanted no part of it. My siblings would remain my father's children forever, twirling to the klezmer music in their magical worlds, doing his bidding.

Syrle never grew up. The juxtaposition of her physical stature and stateliness was in stark contrast to her childlike innocence that never reached her height. There was something inherently childish about my sister. Truly, there had to be, if she could be fooled by our display.

Who wouldn't notice the underlying tension and sadness of our family but a self-absorbed child? I couldn't possibly be like her because I had lost my innocence and I was glad. I didn't want to be like her—utterly indoctrinated, enveloped in comforting lies.

My parents deceived her about my situation because they knew they could. Syrle had none of the mature skills needed to analyze the thick emotions in the room. Whatever she was told, she believed.

On the Sabbath we never discussed business or secular subjects, so I did not have to worry about my sister asking too many questions. Saturday morning, an hour and a half after my father left for synagogue, the four of us walked to services, as I had been doing since I was a child. Being the youngest girl, I used to skip most of the way in my *Shabbos* hat and white gloves. Now, I watched Ella skip while I walked slowly behind, dreading the ordeal at the synagogue.

"Aunt Laya, your sleeves should be longer," my young niece innocently told me as she reached for my elbow.

My mother made a knowing facial expression, but no one other than myself noticed.

As I sat through the service with the other women I felt tormented by my parents' manipulation. But I also felt relief that I had left this stultifying world behind.

For one long, painful weekend, I willingly lived a lie.

I vowed never to do it again.

My new friends asked me constantly why I kept going back. The answer was simple: because I loved them. But loving those who reject you so fully is not possible unless you understand the dynamics of religion, and the brainwashing it requires of its adherents.

Thus, I was absolutely defenseless, a creature so full of love, constantly presented by the virulent behavior toward me. I had no instinct for self-preservation.

So when my beloved, blameless, wounded mother called again, I was not prepared to defend myself.

Mordechai, my beloved younger brother, was getting married.

Now I had to return for my brother's sake.

He had emigrated from the United States to Israel immediately after Seminary and was clueless about my life. He couldn't fathom why I was still not married at twenty-five but kept out of my business.

While stopping by to see our parents before the wedding, he overheard a conversation my father was having with me on the telephone. "Laya, where will you be buried? Did you pick a plot in a Jewish cemetery?"

Mordechai was mortified. "I overheard your conversation. What a terrible thing Dad said to you!" For no valid reason, my brother blamed my father for my not being married. He simply loved me and couldn't figure it out.

Of course, I would attend the wedding in Cleveland and pretend not to be married. What would the bride's family think if his sister didn't attend? Had the community learned of my shameful circumstances, they might judge our family to be unsuitable and call off the wedding entirely.

I had to do this for Mordechai, and then again for my littlest brother Asher. Once they were both married to good matches, my exposure as an unthinkable sinner wouldn't present such dire consequences to their happiness.

More importantly, I knew in my heart of hearts that Mordechai loved me. He would deny me if he knew my situation, he would not be *allowed* to love me, but he still would.

I had so missed Mordechai. Every year, my brother would send me a box of Passover *matzah* that he hand-baked himself in Israel. That box brought back memories of our early morning subway trips the week before Passover to bake *matzah* with my father and our other male relatives in Brooklyn.

We loved those adventures with my father. Of course, Mordechai was the only one who actually got to bake the *matzah*. I was just a girl and not allowed in the room. The girls could not even watch the process, so we played outside.

Now in my seat on the plane, I thought of Mordechai. Growing up we had a close relationship, but at thirteen he had gone off to boarding school and never came back to live at home. He had preferred boarding school to the nightly hours of forced study with my father.

Sitting at the study table, my father would shout at him, "What's the matter with you? Why can't you understand this?" Mordechai, ten years old, would seem to shrink in his seat.

"We just learned it an hour ago," my father would demand. "Let's start again. We're not stopping until you get it right." Determined, he would continue, while my distraught mother went upstairs to her room, closing the door to block out the sound of the bellowing below, while she remained helpless to protect her child.

Sometimes, individuals can teach others skills that they cannot master themselves.

My father had a temper, a rage he could not control. When Mordechai developed temper tantrums in his early years, my father was determined not to pass on his legacy. He showed his son a lifelong lesson through a simple demonstration.

He brought Mordechai to the stove, took a pot from the cabinet, and filled it with milk. He placed the pot on the stove and turned on the gas burner to the highest level of heat. My father let the milk boil hotter and hotter until it rose to the rim and spilled over the sides of the pot. It gushed onto the stovetop, flowed down the oven doors, and created an oozing, sticky mess on the kitchen floor.

As my brother watched in wonderment, my father said, "What you see here is what happens to a person when he loses his temper. If you let it flare and don't contain yourself, you make a mess of life and cause disaster."

His lesson was brilliant. My brother never displayed a temper again.

If only my father could have applied it to his own behavior.

Mordechai's wedding was even more miserable than the earlier charade with Syrle. After the ceremony, the bride's parents had a party at their house. My father rose to give a speech.

To everyone's horror and astonishment, he started on a fiery religious tangent. He didn't mention my name, of course, but I knew his angry words were aimed directly at me. He lectured passionately about Judaism and the need to stay in the fold. He went on and on about our being the chosen nation, his voice rising with inappropriate fervor, every word a bullet to my heart.

Anyone who knew what was going on was paralyzed with fear. Would he expose me in front of all these people? He was completely out of control, so the impossible seemed more and more imminent as his rhetoric continued to accelerate in self-righteous fury.

My brother was white with panic that his father was making a fool out of himself in front of his bride's family, even though he didn't understand why. Yet nobody knew how to stop him.

"We are the Slonimer Dynasty! We come from such greatness! We are a learned family! My grandfather's godliness made his face bright like the sun! We are the chosen people! We are God's people! We are holier than the *Goyim* (non-Jews)!" my father screamed, becoming more and more unhinged.

He was standing in front of all these wedding guests, ranting like a crazy man on a New York street corner that one carefully walks around, eyes down. It was as if he had lost his mind.

Of course, he had lost his mind. He was in agony.

Someone had to do something, and fast.

Candice's husband finally stood and walked to my father's side. Gently, he pulled him away from the podium where he stood and led him to a chair.

Once he sat down, my father stopped talking but he was still beside himself. He had no control, this man who had controlled everything.

When his own mother wanted to remarry, my father said no, and she listened. His sister complied with all of his demands, including changing her own name at his whim. He controlled Candice and Syrle and their families because he supported them. He controlled his employees. And of course, he controlled my mother, who had given up her independence and obeyed his authority.

But he couldn't control me.

PART III

"If I am not for myself, who will be for me?
And being only for myself, what am I?
And if not now, when?"
—Hillel

CHAPTER 27

W E MOVED TO PHILADELPHIA TO BE NEAR JOHN'S FAMILY.
I sold my print shop, tucking the money away for an
eventual down payment on a house. We still had several clients
from the firm in New York, so we rented an office to continue
running our growing data processing company.

At first, to save money, we moved in with John's sister and
her family who lived close to our new office. On the weekends,
we would drive to John's mother's house 85 miles west of
Philadelphia, and live with her. She also owned the house right
next to hers and rented it to tenants.

We did whatever we could to make her life easier: we
painted, made repairs, took care of the lawn, and even put a
new roof on the tenant's house. She saw how happy John and I
were together, and that made her happy.

After five months, we realized it was time to move out
of his sister's home and have our own space, but in order to
continue to put money aside, we decided to live in our office.
We were two of the first tenants in a large new three-story
office building and had three separate rooms. We designed the
space to feel warm and welcoming with the furniture we had
moved from the New York office.

It felt sneaky living there after hours, but it was the smartest
way to have our independence and still prepare for our future.

We slept on the floor in the back room. After all, I could fall asleep in a sleeping bag as easily as I could in a bed. Sleeping on the floor without a pillow every year on the Jewish fast day, *Tishah B'Av*, had been good training, for me. If I had to cook a meal on a hot plate, so be it. Cooked food was still food, regardless of how it was prepared. I was only apprehensive that someone would spot me washing dishes in the bathroom sink.

Late at night, after we finished dinner, I would open the door to the office and look from left to right to see if the cleaning people or anyone else was around. I dashed to the ladies' room and quickly washed the plates, pots, and silverware. Then I would open the bathroom door, peek around the hallway again, and if no one was there, I would scurry back to our office suite, arms loaded. We got ready for bed and crawled into John's green army sleeping bag. For showers, we went to the nearby YMCA, where we had an inexpensive membership.

The mornings, however, were not so easy. I had to dress in the office before going to the ladies' bathroom, just in case a tenant came in early. I could not be seen in a nightgown.

If my family could only see me now, they would be horrified. But John and I didn't see our current living situation as any kind of hardship or shame.

And by now, I deeply understood the value of leaving the safety of my family's cocoon, no matter how powerful and wealthy they were. It was an adventure for us, and we embraced it in that spirit.

We were happy. We were building a life.

I kept discovering new limits from my old world that I hadn't shaken.

I remembered my first time at a formal club event, just after John and I were married. They served huge shrimp on top of crushed ice with a slice of lemon. I was overwhelmed just by looking at it. Scared to death, I thought everyone at the table was watching me. I didn't know if I should use my fingers or a knife and fork.

Shrimp, like all shellfish, bacon, and pork, was *tref*. This meant that, unlike meat and dairy that could be eaten separately but never together, *tref* was absolutely, always forbidden. As an observant child, I was taught that *tref* foods were vile. It was such a terrible sin to eat these foods, that when they were put before you, you wanted to die. You were repulsed at the thought of even seeing these things on a table. The idea of digesting them was physically revolting.

"Just pick it up with your fingers. You'll love it!" John instructed.

Ever so carefully, I picked up one shrimp and squeezed lemon on it to drown out the taste. I put the shrimp in my mouth. It was as if I was eating worms. Imagine if you were told to eat a snake. I was appalled and thought I would choke. It tasted vile. I slipped it into my napkin on my lap. *Non-kosher food is disgusting*, I thought to myself.

I was tasting the brainwashing I had been fed about the evils of *tref*. It was so ingrained in my thoughts, that my mind and body rejected it out of hand.

This was what my family was experiencing when it came to John and me. Utter revulsion. Could they ever overcome their disgust?

To improve our financial situation, a few months later I decided to take a salaried job at Burroughs Corporation (now UNISYS).

The programming staff at my new job was thankfully thirty percent female. It felt much more comfortable, not being the only woman. I certainly didn't enter into any competitions, not even tic-tac-toe.

I loved having the massive computer room almost all to myself, so I started coming in at eleven in the morning and stayed till ten at night. Although we still lived in the office and John was trying to grow the data processing company, it was my salary that sustained us both.

Just a few months later, I was overjoyed to discover that a baby was on its way.

I was nervous that we still didn't have a place of our own. I could not lay on the office floor for the entirety of my pregnancy. We called a realtor, who showed us a half dozen houses. We were uninspired. Finally, he asked if we would consider a piece of land, and drove us to a 13-acre lot on a quiet road.

As we walked around the property, we fell in love with its lushness and possibility. Here was where we could create the exact home we wanted. It just so happened that the lot's owner lived in a house across the street.

What luck!

We quickly wrote up a contract on the hood of the car to take over to him, and he signed then and there. We immediately began construction on the house. We completed whatever related odd jobs we could in order to save on costs and time. John's brother, an electrical engineer, helped him wire the entire house.

The home was built in three months. We moved in just four months before the baby was to be born.

I was so excited to be starting a family of my own because losing contact with my nieces and nephews had been the most devastating part of being rejected by my family. My nieces and nephews had been the joy and love of my life. Before falling asleep I often thought, *I miss them so much.*

I was ready to raise a family in a happy home full of love.

The day before *Yom Kippur*, the holiest day of the Jewish year, our beautiful daughter was born. We named her Raquel Daniela. She was a calm, sweet baby.

When we brought her back to the new house, it seemed surreal. This was what I had waited for my entire life: to marry, raise a family, and be a perfect mother and wife.

For me, being a mother was everything that I'd imagined and more. I loved watching my daughter's small body rise and fall as she slept on my chest, especially in the morning with the warmth of the sunbeams shining on us through the bedroom window.

I loved staring at John when he rocked her to sleep, kissing the top of her head and whispering in her tiny ears how much he loved her.

At the first bird's chirp at dawn, I jumped out of bed to pick her up and cradle her in my arms. She was the softest thing I had ever touched.

Looking down at this precious little treasure of mine, I had a fleeting moment of fright when I thought of how she totally depended upon me.

For the first time in my life, I had complete peace of mind: a husband, a baby, and a happy household filled with love.

And then, the telephone rang.

It was my sister Candice.

Candice was my only sibling who kept in touch with me. Once a year, she would call to say hello and catch up on how I was doing. Later, I would learn that she only called because her *rebbe* instructed her to do so, usually after the private investigator told her of a change in my circumstances.

Her mission was to gauge how likely it was that I might come back. Even though I suspected this, I put it aside and welcomed her calls.

"How are you?" she asked.

"I just had a baby two days ago."

"Oh my. *Mazel tov*. What was it?"

"A little girl."

"May I come to see her?"

I was surprised. "Sure," I said. "Anytime."

The next day, I put on a skirt instead of my usual slacks out of respect for Candice.

I hugged her hello and was surprised that I felt no uneasiness as if we were still the close sisters that we had always been, as though I had just seen her yesterday.

I always felt good in her company. I doubted that she felt comfortable being in my house of sin, but she respectfully took her shoes off upon seeing the sign at the entryway. She sat on the sofa and looked at Raquel, my bundle of joy.

"She's cute."

"Thank you," I said, surprised by the compliment.

"What's her Hebrew name?"

"Daniela. Her name is Raquel Daniela."

I was absolutely going to raise my children in the Jewish culture, and I wanted Candice to see that. I believed that everyone needed an identity, and I wanted my children to be educated and knowledgeable.

John was in complete agreement that we would raise our children in the Jewish faith.

I was still religious and observed the laws. I was even sure my children would grow up and become religious themselves. They would remain in the fold, but eventually, have the freedom to make their own choices.

We sat until late in the afternoon and talked about labor and delivery, the surprises of motherhood, and the joys of being a parent. There was no celebration, no gifts to acknowledge the occasion of my newborn's arrival.

I didn't offer Candice water, as I knew she wouldn't drink it. I didn't offer her food, as I knew she wouldn't permit anything to pass her lips that came from my unclean hands in my unclean house.

I knew she was disappointed that there was now a child, making my seamless transition back to the family impossible. Still, I harbored no ill will toward her.

I felt the unspoken communication of sisters pass between us.

So, it's final, she did not say.

I'm happy. I'm at peace with this child. You cannot sully my happiness, I did not say.

After a few hours, she left without having held Raquel or even having touched her soft, warm cheek. Candice never breathed a word about the birth of my daughter to anyone except her husband. So of course, no one came to welcome my newborn.

When I understood that no contact was forthcoming, I put them out of my mind. I was sure now that Candice had acted correctly in keeping her awareness of my daughter to herself. Knowing about Raquel would devastate my mother. Her hope that I might divorce John kept her from falling to pieces.

Once I had a child, the deal was sealed. Now I couldn't just repent, come back, and marry a respectable yeshiva boy as though nothing had happened.

I decided I would be just fine without my family of origin. To celebrate Raquel's birth, John and I threw our first party in our new, sparkling home. John cooked a fabulous feast, and his entire family came from western Pennsylvania to attend. We talked and laughed all night as everyone fawned over our new baby girl.

John and I were always a team. We hosted many parties in our home. We brought together all the people we loved, creating new traditions that were in stark contrast to the fundamentalist rituals of my childhood.

The most important part was to be free and have fun.

I was determined not to let anything ruin a single moment of the happiness we had built together.

Thirteen months later I was pregnant again, this time with twins. When the delighted doctor announced, "Well, young mother, you are having twins!" I was full of anxiety. I had known twins in my school classes growing up, and disliked the way they were always compared to each other. I was so afraid that my twins would be unfairly judged against each other throughout their lives.

But when Adam and Jacob were born, I took one look at them and all my fears evaporated.

Two magnificent newborns at one time! I marveled at this miracle, in disbelief at my good fortune. I thought to myself, *someday, they will be leaders and right the world's wrongs.* In my mind, I had accomplished the ultimate, greatest feat in world history.

By now, we had cultivated a large community of friends. I was starting to form relationships with people from very different backgrounds. A year earlier I had met Pat, a woman at my sister-in-law's swim club, and we became close. When my sister-in-law told her that I had given birth to twins, Pat set to work making a gallon of vegetable soup.

"It's strictly kosher," she informed my sister-in-law proudly as she handed it over. "No meat, chicken or shellfish!"

It was incredibly considerate of her. Helping one another was how I grew up; this is what the religious community did. I was discovering that one did not have to be religious or godly to do good things.

My parents, of course, still had no knowledge that I was a mother, let alone a mother of three. This pained me, but I accepted their absence as unavoidable, as it was their pain I was focused on preventing. My upbringing had taught me to sacrifice—someone else was always more important than oneself.

Coming from a family as large as mine, it was heartbreaking to reach the ranks of motherhood and have no blood relations to share the experience with.

How sad that they excluded themselves from my life.

When Raquel was born, I left my job at Burroughs to be a full-time, stay-at-home mom.

I considered raising children to be a science, and I wanted *that* to be my job. I had expected that by now, John's business would be able to sustain us all.

It couldn't.

John started his first business with the inheritance money from his ultra-successful father. His father had given him everything. "You'll be college-educated in the best schools. Work for a prestigious company and climb the ladder from there. Having your own business is too stressful," his father wisely advised.

John would hear none of that. Working for someone else was a step down in his mind. Now, however, after years of working in the computer room till midnight to build his business, John had had enough. He simply wanted to work 9-5 and leave whatever was unfinished for the next day. That may be fine when you're working for someone else, but having your own successful business requires a total, unending commitment.

To my disappointment, he was unwilling to work the extra hours necessary to bring in the kind of income that would allow me to stay home with our children. I realized that if we wanted to have a thriving business or any business at all, I would have to be the major income earner.

I began working from home at night. Some nights, I'd take my baby daughter in her wicker basket to the computer room, where we rented computer time to process our jobs, which at times, ran late into the evening. It wasn't ideal, but I knew I could manage. Raquel was a good baby, and I had never minded hard work.

It was the distraction from being a mother that bothered me.

But sometimes in life, we must exchange one good thing for another.

I stood at the door at 5:30 every afternoon, holding Raquel in my arms, waiting for John. "Daddy is coming home soon" I would say with enormous enthusiasm.

We could hardly wait until he came through the front door. John would come home, take off his coat, get on the floor and do nothing but play with Raquel. She crawled on top of him, hugged him, combed his hair—they played for an hour until dinner was ready.

This is what life is really all about, and I cherish those years of love and family. I wouldn't give up those special moments and joys for anything in the world. They were some of the most beautiful years of my life, but I had to give up something for that happiness—and it was worth it.

The treasured vision that I had of being a full-time mom was shattered. Wisely, I decided that there was no time for harping on the negatives. I stayed focused on the steps I needed to take.

After my twins were born, I concentrated on helping John to make our business successful, by selling our data processing services to many Fortune 500 clients. Over time, I built a three-shift operation, to meet the demands.

I created a playroom at the office and brought my children to work with me. I could not bear to leave them with a nanny or put them in daycare.

When they entered grade school, I would work all day but at least I was there to pick them up at 5 from their extended day program (which I and another working parent petitioned the school to start).

The company became more and more successful, but I so wished I could stay at home and raise my children instead of working long days to pay the bills.

When the boys started middle school, I would work until 7:00 pm and make sure to be home at 7:30 pm so we could all sit down to dinner, as a family. Occasionally, it was necessary to go to the other branch of operation in New Jersey and get the second shift started. On those nights, I would return home at 10:00 pm or later.

I wanted my children to have everything, including the knowledge and adventures that were never open to me.

Dedication to hard work allowed me to give them life experiences and educational opportunities they wouldn't have had otherwise. I was able to provide this for them, even though it came at the expense of my dream of being a stay-at-home mom.

Joys and sorrows.

Such is life.

CHAPTER 28

"I MAGINE," SAID PHIL DONAHUE. "TWO COUNTRIES ARE at war, both opposing fundamentalist religions."

While serving breakfast to my children, I'd turned on our kitchen TV to the Phil Donahue show.

Today, he was talking about war. "The religious people on one side are praying to their God to win the war and have God kill off the other side," he continued. "Simultaneously, the religious people in the opposing country are praying to their God to win the war and kill off the people on the other side. Is there only one God? Are both sides praying to the same God? Whose prayers shall God answer?"

A light bulb suddenly went on in my head: people from *all* religions in the world were doing the same thing, praying to the same God, including mine. Who was God to favor? And more importantly, why? Aren't we *all* his children?

I started to grapple with that question, and other ontological questions that I had asked a million times but never had answered.

What would I teach my children?

I wanted to formulate my own views of the world, so I could better guide them. I began to ponder the bigger questions, as philosophers and thinkers had done for thousands of years.

I wanted to focus on what was real. What was here and now, and what we could observe, monitor, and measure.

Did I have a purpose? Could it be defined? I began to think like an independent adult, trying to sort things out without the tutelage of religion.

A local newspaper reporter approached me one day while I was walking out of the post office. "What's your opinion on the draft for our armed forces?"

"I don't believe in the draft, because I don't believe in force," I said with conviction. "Our country should have an army of voluntary young men and women. There's no need for force."

"What if our country was at war?" the reporter asked.

"If America were at war, there would be lines of patriotic volunteers. Look at the lines during World War II, when boys even fudged their ages to enlist to protect our freedom."

The newspaper published my opinion and when I saw it in print, I realized how far I had come not just in living freely, but in thinking and expressing myself freely as well.

In the same newspaper, there was a weekly column that I very much enjoyed, written by a local attorney about his take on politics and issues of the day.

One week, his column included a quote by the author Ayn Rand. I was intrigued by what I read and enthralled to discover someone who thought as I did. I went out the next day and bought a copy of *Atlas Shrugged*.

Ayn Rand was a Russian-American who became famous for her Objectivist philosophy on humankind's role in the world. The title is a reference to Atlas, the mythological Titan, who quite literally holds the world on his shoulders as punishment for angering the gods.

In this novel, one character asks another the advice he would give Atlas. What should the Titan do when "the greater the Titan's effort, the heavier the world bore down on his shoulders"? In other words, what responsibility did Atlas have to the world he held? What responsibility did a person have who was struggling to maintain his individualism over the pressures of collectivism?

What should Atlas do?

The answer was simple: he should shrug.

That is, he should cast off the weight of the world.

I felt my own spirit awaken, as I poured over the pages. The character Atlas embodies the essence of the human spirit. The book's central philosophy is *The concept of man as a heroic being, with his own happiness as the moral purpose of his life, productive achievement as his noblest activity, and reason as his only absolute.*

I had also shrugged. I did not need to bear the weight of my religion, my family, or my Orthodox community. I was responsible for myself, my own happiness; those I had left behind were responsible for theirs. It was my moral obligation to myself not to carry their weight on my shoulders.

Rand made sense out of the world and presented it as knowable. My personal philosophy of life would unfold over time, but it began there.

I went on to read dozens of books on philosophical, cultural, and social issues by Socrates, Plato, Aristotle, Epicurus, Spinoza, Kant, Adams, Churchill, and others.

I began thinking in ways I had never considered before and was never allowed to consider before. All of my youthful fears about God and the world vanished.

Around this time, I started to become *a-religious*. I was still Jewish, historically and culturally. I maintained my religious practices, observed the Sabbath, and kept a kosher home. But the rituals that had been developed over thousands of years began to hold less meaning for me.

I eschewed the fabricated rules. My religious teachings taught me that God put us in this world for only one purpose and that was to serve Him, so we could earn the privilege of access to the *real* world, which comes after this life.

I no longer saw any wisdom in this thinking. Why would a God create people to serve him? Why would he need people in the first place? Was he lonely? If so, how could he be omnipotent? Neither could I comprehend why a supernatural being would produce people, animals, and things just to be destroyed and/ or die, then simply start all over again. For whom? For what?

One by one, I discovered a group of people in Philadelphia who thought the same way I did. I invited them to form a club where we could discuss our viewpoints, and thus the Philadelphia Objectivist Club started.

Robert Finkel, the attorney whose column had started it all, was a founding member. Ed Snider, the owner of the Philadelphia Flyers hockey team, was also an admirer of Ayn Rand and let us use his office for club meetings.

Reading Rand and talking with like-minded people inspired me to shed undeserved guilt.

I would continue to move forward, unencumbered by my past. I had a new quest to live life to the fullest.

CHAPTER 29

Like Sisyphus, condemned for eternity to roll the mythological boulder up the hill over and over again, my father would send many delegates to bring me back to the fold, and like the labors of Sisyphus, his efforts would be futile.

Before I married John, I would often visit Montreal to see my sister Marilyn and her children. A friendship developed between Marilyn's best friend, Hannah, and myself.

Twelve years after I married John, the phone rang out of the blue.

"How are you? Do you remember me? It's Hannah. Marilyn finally relented and gave me your phone number and told me where you live. For ten years I had been questioning her for information about you, but she would never tell me what happened or where you were. Can I come to see you? I just landed at the Philadelphia Airport."

I was delighted and quickly drove to pick her up. Hannah was wonderful, and she made me feel wonderful, too. At home, she immediately fell in love with my children. She was nonjudgmental, a welcome change. When John came home from work, she accepted him immediately. That first visit and every visit thereafter, she stayed in our guest room.

Hannah was the only person from my past who treated John with respect. She was an ultra-religious Orthodox Jewish woman who had the capacity to see beyond our differences and befriend my entire family. She loved my children, and when Raquel was eleven she went with her to Florida to celebrate the Passover holiday.

Many years later, I would discover that Hannah was being paid for all those visits. I had always wondered how she had the funds to travel to and from Canada and buy the expensive gifts she used to bring us. Whatever genuine feelings she may have had for us, ultimately she was just another spy sent by my father.

He never stopped trying to gather information on me, to discover some doubt or unhappiness that could be exploited to compel me to return. This betrayal is still difficult to accept. I thought she was the one exception, falsely believing that she could love God, my family, and me at the same time.

Other people from my past occasionally appeared when I'd least expect them. One afternoon, my babysitter Mrs. Barker, who adored my children, called me at work. Frantic and so flustered, I could barely understand her.

I could hear the fear in her voice. "A woman from Israel is here. She's wearing a turban on her head! I told her she couldn't come into the house, but she literally pushed herself through the door.

"She's stronger than I am and I couldn't stop her! Do you know this woman? She refuses to leave. What should I do? What if she grabs the children—are they safe?"

The turban was the giveaway.

Aunt Dee Dee never thought it was proper to wear a wig. To her, covering your hair was not about replacing it with more beautiful hair that looked real. She was Uncle Nathan's wife, and also ran an organization to rescue so-called lost Jewish girls in Jerusalem.

She was tough, a self-assured, unstoppable woman who intimidated her students and made her own rules. As the wife of a famous and revered *Rebbe*, she had status.

Mrs. Barker stayed with the children while I took my aunt for a drive.

"The community wants you back. You could have a great life if you left John and returned to us," Aunt Dee Dee said matter-of-factly as she climbed into the passenger seat of my car and buckled her seatbelt.

"In fact, you really are not married. It's not possible for a Jewish girl to be married to a non-Jewish man. You are just living in sin." She smiled in her charming way. "I came to teach you how to repent and come back to your senses. You still have a chance to go to heaven. God will forgive you."

I was startled and truly did not know what to say. As we drove through the wooded residential roads of suburban Philadelphia, Aunt Dee Dee and I began to talk about philosophy, which led us to the topic of selfishness.

She said, "If you do something nice for someone and you derive pleasure from it, you're being selfish. It may be constructive, but nevertheless, it's a form of selfishness."

I had never thought in such terms before: that kindness and doing good deeds could be selfish. Was Aunt Dee Dee being selfish right now, smug and sure in her mission to rescue me? Imagine her joy if she succeeded! Did this make her a selfish person?

My mind began turning the idea over, comparing my aunt's ideas to what I had learned from Ayn Rand's philosophy. For Rand, rational selfishness was a virtue because pursuing happiness should be your highest aim, as long as you did so with the regard of others.

Aunt Dee Dee went on, telling me that there was a higher virtue in sacrifice, in the form of the rational observance of rituals of self-abnegation, to give up one's own desires to fulfill others. Jewish scholars teach that suffering is the characteristic feature of religion. In essence, pain helps us focus on self-improvement.

But here was Aunt Dee Dee, grinning by my side, any pain she felt about my situation eclipsed by her joy in her "good deed." She was, at this very moment, fulfilling Rand's highest moral aim: her own happiness. Like my Uncle Nathan, she was happiest when she was "rescuing" a wayward Jew.

And yet, I should return to a world of suffering and be grateful for it?

Driving along with my aunt beside me, rattling on about why I should come home to the family and accept my suffering as good, only gave me one more reason why I should not. I had parented my own children, pioneered my own business, and made my own close friends.

I had become a person who asked questions and demanded rational answers. Talking to Aunt Dee Dee had revealed how few answers she actually had, how flawed and hypocritical her thinking was. I was happy that I could see reason through the cracks in her logic.

She returned to Jerusalem and I returned unrepentant to my beautiful home and children.

Outwardly I brushed off Aunt Dee Dee's visit, but in truth, it stirred memories of my former life that I had been able to bury until then. In revisiting those moments, I realized that my childhood was full of situations where my parents treated me as if my feelings didn't matter.

These upsetting experiences, normally involving my body, would not have been terrifying if they had just taken the time to be honest with me.

I remembered going to the doctor when I was six. "I'm not getting a shot today, right Mommy?"

"No, not today. Just a checkup."

In the office, while my mother and the doctor's own young daughter looked on, the doctor forced down my pants and pushed the needle into my buttock.

Humiliation and betrayal shot through me as surely as if they had been the contents of the doctor's syringe. It was so unfair, so inappropriate—and my mother watched, looking at me as if I were inconsequential.

My mother had lied.

She knew I was getting a shot and she lied. To her, I was just a child. I didn't have feelings. I wasn't important, so why not lie? Why not pull my pants down in front of a stranger?

More miserable recollections of shame surfaced. My parents were on their yearly vacation and my grandmother had come to take care of us. I was seven, maybe eight. At night, I had to take a bath. The maid was in the bathroom with us. My grandmother told me to take my clothes off. I didn't want to be naked in front of the maid, a stranger.

"Just do it. We have to get going."

And so I did. Shamed and disrespected again.

Why was this memory causing me so much pain now? Back then, it certainly caused me pain, but I wasn't allowed to feel it because I wasn't allowed to have feelings. Now, I felt it full force.

The final, most prominent memory came back to me. I was eighteen, unmarried, living with my parents. My mother insisted that I go to the doctor to get a checkup, even though there was nothing wrong with me.

The doctor told me to go into the bathroom, take my panties off, and leave my slip-on. My mother stayed in the examination room. She and the doctor talked about me as if I was not there.

I was so relieved I could at least wear my slip, but then the doctor said, "Lie down. Spread your legs." He was looking at my vagina. My mother was standing there. I was nothing. I was a non-entity.

It was just horrible. I think back now: did my mother take my brothers to the doctor and stand by while he looked at their private parts? Did she do it to my sisters? I don't think she did it to them. My sister Marilyn certainly would have told me. I didn't know what to make of it.

The disrespect stays with you. It doesn't leave your psyche.

I was angry. Furious. My own mother? Why didn't she protect me? Why didn't she care?

A lifetime of brainwashing and repression slowly began to fall away.

The moments a child remembers most are the ones their parents failed to protect them. I wouldn't be that parent. I was determined to protect my children from anyone and everything unjust. I would not deceive them. I didn't accept the idea that a child should suffer.

CHAPTER 30

IT WAS A BRIGHT SUNNY MORNING, A NEW DAY. I COULD sense the energy, see the soft blue of the sky, and feel the slight breeze in the air. I stepped outside and took a deep breath. I stretched out my arms, lifted my face to the sky, and felt the warm sun all over my body.

"Come on outside," I called to the children through the screen door. "Let's play hopscotch. It's gorgeous out here." They came running out, excited to have fun.

The telephone rang. I heard John grab it and speak briefly with the caller. He came into the backyard and interrupted our game of hopscotch. "Someone named Rose is on the phone."

To my delight, it was one of my father's cousins, Shani. Shani was short for Shoshana, meaning *rose* in Hebrew. She was the daughter of my grandmother's sister. "I finally found you. Do you know who I am?" The unmistakable high-pitched voice on the other end of the phone could only be Shani's. Suddenly, the house seemed even brighter, the colors of our garden even more beautiful than just a moment before.

Shani was twenty years younger than my father and a generation older than me. But she was youthful in her outlook and demeanor. She dressed in clothes that revealed a curvaceous body and loved to make heads turn as she walked. When I was a young religious girl, it made me very uncomfortable when Shani came to visit dressed like that. I would stare at her out of the corner of my eye and quickly look away. Now I embraced her just as she was.

I had always liked my cousin—the very one my father used to lecture me about because she was unmarried and "wasting her life" with a career. I had only seen her on a few occasions as I was growing up because she and her mother were not considered religious enough. Consequently, I never confided in Shani after meeting John, and she knew nothing about my three children. Now, it was a beautiful and welcome connection.

"Of course, I remember you. It's so good to hear your voice. How is Aunt Esther?"

"Actually she's the one who insisted I find out where you are. She said she didn't care what you had done, or where you are. Just to find you. Mama remembers how you visited her every Saturday for years while she was sick. Your mother still doesn't say a word when someone asks for you. In fact, everyone is afraid to ask. No one knows where you are. You simply disappeared without a trace."

Shani had persisted in trying to obtain my phone number. Since mother held firm, she finally went to my sister Candice, who gave in.

"Candice told me that you have children! I want to hear all about your life."

"Of course!" I was so eager to connect.

After her call, Shani visited our family a half-dozen times a year, and it was no wonder my children adored her. "Let's cuddle up on the sofa together," she would gush as she enthusiastically invited all three of them onto her lap. They would make a dash to squeeze in for Aunt Shani's bundles of hugs and kisses. She loved my children and told them wildly embellished fairy tales, while they hung off her every word. "Say it again!" they cried, and doubled up with laughter at the outrageous details she added.

As I watched Shani interact with my children, it brought back the many loving memories I had of her dear mother. Aunt Esther, my grandmother's sister, had emigrated from Israel with the help of my father. She was my only aunt who was culturally Jewish but not religious. She was also the only aunt that I genuinely loved. I admired her courage and was amazed at how hard she worked to support her family. Her husband Joseph was a frail man but a highly intelligent Ph.D. He was one of those people who could never earn an adequate living, but always had an excuse for why the job did not work out. It fell on my Aunt Esther to support him and their three children, so she purchased a building two blocks from the bay, in the town next to my parents, and turned it into a rooming house that she ran herself.

On those special occasions when Mother brought us to visit Aunt Esther, we stood outside her three-story rooming house on the sidewalk where we could see the water, feel the wind, and hear the waves on the beach.

Mother would knock on the door and Aunt Esther would come out with an apron tied around her plump body. "Hi, hi, hi! Come on in!" As we walked into the entryway she would gush, "Come over here and let me give you a hug!" Aunt Esther was always loving and generous with us, enveloping us in big hugs where we melted into her soft, warm body. It was the only time we felt cherished by an adult, and ever so strongly. She bought boxes of Hershey chocolates and tried unsuccessfully to sneak the bars to us, knowing full well that my mother would object. Mother immediately took hold of them and gave us *one* square each. She promised my Aunt Esther she would give us more later on. Somehow at home, after those marvelous visits, the chocolates had a way of disappearing, never to be seen again.

Aunt Esther was also a wonderful baker, but because she was not deemed religious enough, we were not allowed to eat in her home. The fresh-baked pastries always smelled so good. We weren't allowed to say a word about that, but no one could stop me from *wishing*. Years later, as a sixteen-year-old, at one family function, I unwittingly picked up one of her delicious pastries, and as I put it in my mouth, my mother whispered in my ear, "Aunt Esther made those, and we can't trust her *kashrus* (how kosher she was)." Feeling guilty and confused, and against my better judgment, I removed the *rugelach* from my mouth. I felt a lump in my throat. I said to myself, *How un-kosher could this be? It's just a piece of pastry.*

Now as Shani and I relived old memories, she told me they had heard and seen it all—Mother whispering, my taking the cake out of my mouth. She said it humiliated them, and I was again reminded of the senseless pain that religious fervor could inflict.

I was in my early 20s and still living at home when my mother and I would visit Aunt Esther each weekend. We would see firsthand how tenderly Shani took care of her ailing mother, every weekend for five years. She colored and styled her hair and manicured her nails, to make Aunt Esther feel pretty. She made sure her mother had every comfort and performed these services with loving cheer.

As we walked back home from one of our Saturday afternoon visits, my mother took me by surprise when she voiced her private thoughts.

"I wonder what will happen to Shani?" my mother mused aloud. "She doesn't obey the Ten Commandments, she violates the Sabbath, doesn't eat strictly kosher, and yet the way she cares for Aunt Esther must deserve some reward in heaven. What will happen to her?"

I wondered the same thing. Does her kindness count for nothing, will she have no reward in the world to come, because she's not a Sabbath observer? It seemed very unfair. But we both let those thoughts fall by the wayside instead of exploring that troublesome incongruity.

Shani began to celebrate the major holidays with us, and even though I had become non-observant, I still looked forward to celebrating the Jewish holidays with our family and those we loved. Always wearing glamorous clothing, Shani arrived with a bright, wide smile. The children could not wait to open the door and find her standing there with a pie box in hand.

"Who wants banana cream pie?" she would squeal with delight. She brought one on every visit. I didn't know who was more excited—the children or Aunt Shani. It went without saying that we were all permitted to eat every delicious, made-with-love bite.

John, who had learned to sail during his college years, was finally able to fulfill his lifelong dream and buy a racing boat that we as a family could enjoy. We owned a cabin cruising sailboat and kept it at the club we belonged to on the Long Island Sound. John named it *Poseidon (God of the Seas)*. We spent most of our summer weekends living on the boat and sailing along the Connecticut coastline. On many weekends, Shani would join us, to the delight of all.

On the occasional visits Shani had with my mother, the topic of discussion was always the same: "How can we get Laya to come back?" My mother repeatedly relived my departure and could not come to terms with it. She knew that Shani kept in touch with me, and was one of the few people with whom she could share her distress.

"How did this happen?" my mother would ask.

Shani would console her. "She's happy with her life."

It was during one of their conversations that Shani, unaware that she was breaking a confidence, let my biggest secret slip.

"All three children are so adorable," she said, offhandedly. At that time, the twins were five and Raquel was seven.

My mother looked at her, aghast. She could not believe that I had three children. Traumatized, she began to sob.

My mother wanted to see her grandchildren.

CHAPTER 31

I ARRIVED AT PENN STATION IN MANHATTAN AT 1:30 ON A Tuesday afternoon. Stepping onto the platform with a heavy heart, I wondered anxiously about my mother's state of mind. All these years I tried so hard to protect her from pain. Now that she knew I had three children, my mother's hope of getting her Laya back to marry a fine Jewish boy had vanished. Without that hope, would she ever recover?

My head was racing.

As hundreds of passengers rushed by, I noticed a frail woman wrapped in a heavy winter coat sitting next to my sister, Candice.

With a jolt, I realized that the old woman was my mother.

Where was the self-assured, energetic woman who raised me? I could barely walk to the bench. My mother's eyes were red and swollen from crying. *You will be like Leah in the Bible with puffy eyes if you continue to cry.*

A vision from the past filled my mind: I was eight years old, it was during one of our Saturday afternoon meals, and I was crying for some now-long-forgotten reason. My mother looked at me and said, "Rita, if you continue to cry, your eyes will be red and you will look like Leah in the bible." Her words jolted me to the core. I knew all of the Bible stories by heart, but this one was particularly meaningful to me because it was about *my* Hebrew namesake, *Leah*. Leah was not pretty, so she cried, thinking she would never get a husband. "Don't cry, or you will be like Leah."

A great fear took hold of me. I didn't want to be like Leah, with red, puffy eyes and no husband. I wanted to be like Rachel, Leah's sister, who was beautiful and loved by Jacob.

I would never cry again. I was a child who did what she was told. While some read the Bible story of Leah as allegory, I took it literally.

What had I done? If only I could take it back, start all over, and see her happy face, her strong, determined soul again. I recalled one of her letters: *all of my joys have sullied since you left. Come back to us, make me whole again.*

I knew that people thought I had destroyed her life. Now, seeing her, I wondered if they were right.

My sister whispered to her. My mother looked up, saw me, and started crying again. I hurried over and gave her a long hug, bringing on another flow of tears.

"Hi, Mom." Only a whisper came out.

"Mommy is very upset." Candice put her arm around my mother protectively. "This is what you've done to her. She can't cope with this."

Another stab through the heart. I willed myself not to break down.

When my mother was able to regain her composure, she said, "Shani told me that you have three children. I'm sure that it was difficult for you to keep this a secret." Her voice quivered. "I would like to meet them."

I was so happy to hear those words. Even though my mother had *forty-nine* other grandchildren, if she wanted to meet mine then they still meant something to her. She had noted my sacrifice in not telling her for so many years. And her willingness to see them meant that our shared humanity overcame religious dogma. If a relationship between my children and their grandparents was conceivable, then what else was possible?

Was it possible that my children could be accepted into the family?

My memory of the rest of that visit is blurred. I can only remember sitting by her, both of us engulfed in sadness, Candice watching and silently judging, while my mother and I made plans for me to bring the children to my family's home in Long Island.

A few weeks later, I woke up early to prepare for the trip. John was not welcome in my parents' home and not a part of this significant, yet terrifying, day. I was relieved.

After packing bags for me and the children, I set bowls of cereal in front of them. Then I explained to them once again our outing. "We're going to New York so you can meet your grandparents for the first time."

The children ate quietly, considering this remarkable news. Prior to that day, I had never talked about my parents. Because of their young ages, and because John's mother and Shani were so wonderful to them, they felt no lack of familial love, and the topic had simply never come up. Perhaps they were thinking about what it would be like to finally have a grandfather. Perhaps they were just bewildered that I hid this from them. They could tell that I wasn't myself.

I was sad and quiet, unable to put my feelings in order, to make sense of any of it. How would they take to their grandparents? Would my parents be happy to see them, or would our visit just make them feel even more hopeless?

The drive up the turnpike was quiet. I was at a loss for words and was surprised my children were as well. I had always assumed their lives were full, with our family-by-choice and the many friends they had. They had a wonderful *Nonna* and were not bereft of grandparenting love. I saw no reason to tell them that in the world they were about to enter, they were less significant and damned to eternal hellfire because their father was not Jewish.

They had no idea of the history of events that led up to this fraught rendezvous. But they had picked up on my emotions, and unable to understand them were reacting with caution.

A slew of memories surfaced as I turned the car into my old street and pulled up to the big stone house. I remembered snow days as a child when it would snow so much that school was cancelled. My mother did not relish the prospect of having all six of her children bouncing around the house all day, and neither did she want us to make a snowy mess of her pristine carpets. So, we were bundled up and shoved out into the elements, and told we weren't allowed back in the house until lunchtime. I would stand shivering in the cold, and my hatred of being put out in the snow made it feel even colder.

I remembered the all-day baseball games; walking up the path hand-in-hand returning from the synagogue, and the endless, awkward dates streaming in and out of that heavy wooden door.

I remained calm, determined to maintain my composure as the four of us walked up the familiar walkway. It was not an easy task. The house looked the same from the outside, but through the eyes of my children, it was brand new.

"You lived here?" Jacob asked with wonder.

"I did," a little stunned myself that I was about to enter this place again, something I hadn't considered possible just a few weeks before.

I went to ring the doorbell, but before I pushed the button the door opened—they had been watching us from the window.

Candice had opened it. My parents stood behind her.

I gave my mother a hug. To my father, I said simply "Hi, Dad." I turned to the children.

"This is your grandma and your granddaddy. And this is your Aunt Candice."

My mother stepped forward. She bent toward the children and hugged them warmly. To my relief, they responded in kind. My father smiled as well, making him appear cheerful, friendly, and caring.

Maybe, just maybe, this was all going to turn out okay.

My mother straightened, but not to her usual grand self. It was a subtle but devastating difference, her ordinariness. The self-assured woman I had known was not standing in that vestibule. She had always been cheerful when I came home from the office, and especially when her grandchildren came running in the house shouting, "Hi Grandma!"

Now, I could see the fear in her eyes: *Here they are, these children, and now all is lost. They will not be accepted into heaven. What have I done? What can I do? Nothing.*

My mother smiled through her pain and fooled my children with the facade she was presenting. It was a supreme kindness that the children didn't know her well enough to sense anything wrong. My mother gaily ushered everyone into the kitchen where we found gifts and sweets waiting on the table. My children were shy, but the candy and the new surroundings excited them.

I, on the other hand, was looking past the sweets to the religious propaganda taped to the cabinets and over the sink. Cloying pictures of *rebbes,* and framed, bible quotes in Hebrew had joined the always-present words of my youth that hung over the sink, *Time Is a Terrible Thing to Waste.*

How much time we had wasted apart! And what had happened during that time? My tasteful mother taping up these cultish posters in her house was shocking, another sign of the fear that had overtaken her. *She cannot let my children come for Sabbath; she cannot bring them to her synagogue, because she cannot say "these are my grandchildren"; she has to hide them in this kitchen; she has to hide herself from the shame of their existence.*

Adam whispered to me, "Can we see your room?"

"Sure, I'll show you the whole house."

I was overtaken by emotion at seeing the rooms I had so loved as a child: the comfort and privacy of my blue room where I could always escape, the gaiety of the kitchen where we baked cookies on holidays, and the warmth of the dining room where we had our Sabbath meals. As the children peeked in every room, my mother followed closely and spoke lovingly to them. The children took to her immediately.

They did not gravitate toward my father. The boys especially felt uncomfortable and anxious in his presence. He invited the twins into his study. As soon as a young boy could talk, my father felt it was his duty to indoctrinate him with religious teachings. The twins had no idea what to make of this. Clinging to me with their little hands, they whispered, "Stay with us, Mommy." I remained with them in the dining room while my mother went into the kitchen to show Raquel the little heart-shaped cookie cutters she used to make sugar cookies. Being a girl, my daughter was not expected to study the Talmud with her brothers, so she was excused from my father's overbearing presence.

My mother, on the other hand, was winning over Raquel and vice-versa. I'm sure it was bittersweet for my mother. On the one hand, Raquel was a delight, just the kind of sweet, respectful child my mother loved and admired. On the other hand, she was a product of her Christian father.

Candice stood guard, ready to jump in if the situation became overwhelming for my mother. During my absence, Candice had assumed the burden of taking care of her, as my other siblings lived out of the country. Mother had cried a lot over the years, and Candice was the only one left to comfort her.

I was grateful that she had been there for our mother when I wasn't, but I could not forgive her for not bringing her children to this visit. *Was my body made of steel, to take these punches and have them bounce right off my back? My children were meeting their grandparents and their aunt, for the very FIRST time! But where are their cousins? Do my children not mean anything to Candice? How I loved my own nieces and nephews. How I showered them with love. Is it too dangerous for her children to meet their cousins? After all, they were Jewish cousins, too. How degrading, how humiliating! She is excommunicating my three, innocent, lovely children. It was all about God in heaven, we here on earth are meaningless.*

I had known her older children from the moment they were born, and spent so much time caring for and playing with them. I would spend hours with Candice's three oldest boys at their neighborhood playground.

I showered my nieces and nephews with presents, I took them on special trips to Manhattan, I loved to smile and laugh with them. After I left, all of this joy was abruptly cut out of my life. I was forbidden from contacting any of them.

I'm not sure why I thought this, but I imagined that even though they meant the world to me, my departure wouldn't affect them. Years after I left, I was surprised and heartbroken to learn that this wasn't the case, in a letter I received from Candice's daughter:

> *Dear Aunt, Laya (may G-d let you live),*
>
> *This may be the first letter that you're getting from me, but let me tell you, it's not the 1st, 2nd, or 3rd that I have already written to you. I wrote so many letters, but I didn't know if you would want to receive them. This time, I'm sending it anyway and I do hope that you are happy to hear from me.*
>
> *I don't know how to start, but let me just tell you: I MISS YOU SO MUCH & I ALWAYS THINK OF YOU! I remember you so clearly at night before I go to sleep and I always wish that I could see you—just to say hi—and to see you smile at me. Remember when you bought my brothers their speed bikes? What about your tan car w/ a sunroof (You may not remember it but I do—your visits were not forgotten too quickly!) I can still picture you wearing your rain hat, white on the brim with light transparent colored circles. Am I right, do you remember it? Is your hair still long?*
>
> *Aunt Laya, please come visit.... Do you think about me? Do you want to see me as much as I want to see you?*

Mazel tov on Solomon's engagement! Aunt Laya, you must come to my brother's wedding (such a, thank God, happiness.) The Bride is such a sweet, lively, adorable, pretty girl. They'll make the cutest couple. They both talk non-stop about the other. Yup, that is your little nephew.

Aunt Laya, you never saw my two little brothers. Aunt Laya, you never saw your little nephew, "Davis", NEVER. Can you please come? Come see Ben and Manasseh, and the wedding will be on December 25. If you come, Aunt Laya, ask anything from me.

My watch says 12:35 after midnight, the house is sleeping, though Tatty (father in Yiddish) is not home yet and I have so much more to say. But the only reason why I'm writing is b/c I really miss you and I really wish I could see you!

Good night, Aunt Laya....

Thanks a lot for reading the letter.

I hope I have the courage to send this one.... But, HOW MUCH LONGER DO I HAVE TO WAIT: 11 years? Or are 9 years enough?!?!

Love, your niece,
Leeann (written when she was 17 years old)

On later visits when I came with my children, Candice hid her two youngest, who were too little to be left at home, in her car. She could acknowledge to her nine children that non-Jews populated the rest of New York, the country, and the world. However, she could not admit that her sister had committed the mortal sin of marrying outside of the Jewish religion.

I should have called her openly on it, right in front of our mother. Right then and there, we should have had a frank conversation. *Why didn't you bring your children to see their cousins? Why are you hiding your children from mine? Are we contaminated? Are you afraid that your children might see upstanding children that are not religious?*

In my family's eyes, intentionally raising children without two completely devoted, highly religious Orthodox Jewish parents was a crime against nature. If they discovered that my children were not unrighteous, but actually loving and kind people, it would disprove their worldview and possibly poison their young minds that religion does not define one's goodness or character.

But the confrontation was not in my nature. It has, unfortunately, taken far too long for me to realize the error of my ways. In retrospect, I know that I could not expect her to change if I kept quiet and did not address her actions.

Marilyn behaved the same way. She had twelve children. Never once did she care to meet my children when she came to visit my parents, who lived only two hours away from me. My children were excommunicated as long as they had a non-Jewish father.

After I had married John but before Raquel had been born, she came to see my parents with her four children, one of whom was a baby. When I went to hold her baby, she stopped me. "I'll take him. He needs a nap." I recognized then that I was a tainted woman and she wanted no bad omen to befall her child.

Shortly after our first trip to see my parents, Mordechai came back to America with his family and wanted to see me and meet my children. When I brought Raquel and the twins to my parents' house, he had arranged for his children to have a playdate elsewhere.

I was not capable of expressing anger at them. He and his wife showered my children with games and candy whenever we went to see them at my parent's house.. I had the urge to hand back the gifts. *It is not gifts that we need*, I longed to say. *Give of yourself and your families*. But I was too accommodating. I stood there passively every time, watching the transactions. They wanted to be able to embrace my children but just couldn't disobey the rigid rules that were the bedrock of their lives.

His children wore *pe'us* (long sidelocks deemed necessary from a single line in Leviticus), all-black suits, fur hats, high white socks, and full beards. This manner of dress harkens back to the style of Polish nobility in the sixteenth century, before the birth of Hasidism. My brother and his sect would sweat through humid New York summers or under the scorching Israeli sun dressed like men from medieval Poland because generations before them and the people around them did it.

Their attempts to buy Raquel, Adam, and Jacob's love with treats and sweets, to bribe them into fundamentalist Judaism, had no hope of success. They did not need *things*. They responded to sincere affection and warmth.

Regrettably, the family's love was conditional. It was predicated upon the acceptance of their dogmatic form of Judaism, their constricted way of life, and my children's abandonment of their father. Candice told me that children had no obligation to a father who was a non-Jew, and so renouncing him would be a reasonable demand.

When we ended these visits, Candice would walk us to the door, and while my mother hugged the children, I'd promise to come back again.

Candice would wait until we got into the car and then close the door behind us.

I couldn't get away fast enough. I would drive without looking back, feeling I'd escaped another ordeal. These visits, and the pain which accompanied them, were deeply etched into my being.

I would later hear a story about my mother hearing of a child who had been diagnosed with cancer. "I don't know who has it *worse*," my mother had said to her friend. She was, of course, thinking of me. To her, it was as painful to have a child who had married a non-Jew as it was to have a child with a terminal disease. In fact, her situation was even more heartbreaking. At least with illness, she could not be blamed for failing as a parent.

CHAPTER 32

I_N 1989, ^{MY} ^{DAUGHTER} ^{HAD} ^{HER} B^{AT} M^{ITZVAH}. H^{ERE} ^{SHE} was, barely a teenager, about to claim her place in the world of young Jewish women. After school, I carpooled with other parents to take her and the twins to Hebrew classes. Each child understood that they could make their own decisions about religion when they were grown.

Typically, parents of Bar or Bat Mitzvah candidates will write most of their child's speech, spend hours studying with them, and hire private tutors to help them learn their portion in the Torah scrolls. Some start preparing their children as early as three years prior to the event, to show them off. I did none of this. I sent Raquel to Hebrew school and had full confidence that she would be prepared.

I was amazed at her performance. At the Friday night service, she stood with the Rabbi in front of the whole congregation and led the entire service, in Hebrew, by herself. I treasured this chance to stop and stare in awe at my daughter. I was so proud that she had learned all of this by herself and that she had *chosen* to learn it.

The following Saturday morning, Raquel once again led the services, on her own, reading ancient prayers and passages from the Torah Scroll with complete confidence. After the reading, Raquel stood on the *bimah* (the altar) and gave her Bat

Mitzvah speech. She was becoming a scholar, participating in an event that in my previous world only boys had access to.

Before congratulating Raquel on her Bat Mitzvah, the Rabbi turned to the congregation. "All members of the family, please rise." Other than my cousin Shani, whom I was thrilled to see, no one else from my biological family was there to witness this occasion.

I looked out over the congregation, seeing Shani standing alone. I tried to contain the hurt and the ache of my missing parents, sisters, brothers, nieces, and nephews. *This is a happy day*, I reminded myself, trying to convince myself that I didn't need them or their approval and neither did Raquel.

Then John's mother, Raquel's beloved Nonna, stood. My heart expanded with joy. To my children, she was the equivalent of two grandmothers and two grandfathers. She gave them more than all four ever could have combined.

John's sister and her family proudly rose. Next his brother with his family followed. Then my friend Trish and her husband stood along with their daughter, whose Bat Mitzvah we had attended the previous year.

One by one, each member of my chosen family rose to stand with us, proud participants in my child's journey.

And that is what life is about. Family.

Raquel shone like a star. At the Bat Mitzvah candle-lighting ceremony, she lit the first candle. John and I lit the second. Then the twins each lit a candle. Each member of our chosen family was called up to light a candle and say Congratulations.

I no longer felt alone. We were family regardless of whom we decided to marry, which religion we believed in, what our personal relationship with God might be, or how we decided to dress. We shared a true, lasting bond that came from sharing the same values, and not because we were indoctrinated with those values as children, but because we had chosen them as adults, each of us in our own time and in our own way.

I was surrounded by love.

CHAPTER 33

WHEN I ENTERED THE SECULAR WORKING WORLD IN 1968, I found that there were rules for everyone but again the women's rules were more restrictive. There were separate men's and women's sections in the Help Wanted ads, where only particular jobs were available to women. Women were tacitly forbidden from wearing pants to their office jobs, where they were paid much less than men. The justification for this was that men needed to support their families, and women did not. Young women weren't considered for certain significant positions at their jobs because they would marry, become pregnant, and then leave to raise a family, or so the thinking went. Men had the freedom to buy whatever they wanted with cash or credit, while women were not allowed to hold credit cards and needed their husbands or fathers to cosign a loan application.

The dictionary defines feminism as the belief that women and men should have equal rights economically, politically, and socially. By this definition only, I would be considered a feminist.

On my first official sales call as a young businesswoman, I visited a hospital in Long Island to pitch our data processing services to the purchasing director. Because I did data processing myself and wasn't just a salesperson, I gave very thorough and convincing presentations. I described the advantages of working with our company and our impressive client list. I showed him a beautifully printed proposal outlining our services and costs. The director was impressed and told me so. "You are the most qualified of all the vendors, but quite frankly, you won't be awarded the contract because you're a woman."

Shedding tears would have been a sign of weakness. I did not throw a fit, rant or rave—nor did I sue the hospital, I simply moved on to the next prospect. I knew that I offered the best services at a good price and understood data processing better than anyone else, so I remained confident that the sales would start to come in, and soon after they did.

Starting my own company in New York was the best decision I ever made. I answered only to myself and hired a team of competent employees. After moving to Philadelphia years later, I reached a certain level of success. I was then invited to join the Forum for Executive Women, an organization of women in local positions of leadership, and I accepted.

At our entrepreneurial round tables, we were able to compare experiences and help each other solve challenges. It inspired progress toward a world in which women and men share an equal place in leadership.

In 1993, I was invited to join The Union League of Philadelphia. It was formed in 1862 to support President Lincoln and his goal of preserving the Union. It is currently the number one business club in the country.

All of Philadelphia's top law firms, banks, and corporations are represented there. I knew that my involvement with this prestigious organization would strengthen my position in the business community. As important, I admired the club's focus on patriotism.

Over the years, the League expanded its membership to accept all individuals; it took until August of 1986 for female members to be allowed. After two "no" votes earlier in the 1980s, a faction of men threatened to leave the League unless a majority voted to admit female members. For the first time, red power dresses could be found amidst the gray suits. The Union League would no longer be known as the private club with a separate basement entrance for the members' wives.

Before I became a member, I would visit the League with John. Its style of decoration reminded me of our past trips to the similarly stately Seawanhaka Corinthian Yacht Club, one of the oldest yacht clubs in the Western Hemisphere. John joined this male-only membership club shortly before we married. One afternoon, I walked into the bar and sat down on a bench, just to observe the splendid room, not to order a drink.

A few minutes later, John came up to me and whispered in my ear, "You're not allowed in this room, someone is complaining."

Utterly bewildered, I asked. "Why not?"

"Only men are allowed in the bar," he answered sheepishly. That was not acceptable to me. I stayed put, shocked by the childishness of it all.

That night I wrote a letter to the president of the club, recounting my experience that day. "It reminds me of when I was a little girl and the boys didn't allow us in their clubhouse!"

The following month, Seawanhaka Corinthian Yacht Club removed the restriction.

When members join the League, they are invited to join club tables—clubs within the club. These tables are the key to getting to know what each mini-club offers and bonding with like-minded friends in the League. My preference was to join the "12:30 Table", because I knew some of those members. My husband was invited to join, but I wasn't, so I asked to join and was told that it was a male-only table. I tried two others—the same result.

I felt the lack of a women-only table; specifically, a place where dynamic, entrepreneurial women could meet and make meaningful connections. I met with the chair of the club tables. He was delighted, a little startled and intrigued, by the idea of a club table made up solely of women. The following year, the One Percenters club table was official.

The charter members consisted of self-made female entrepreneurs: CEOs, presidents, executives, and founders of banks, IT companies, and more. The accomplished women of the League now had a table to call their own, where they could enjoy lively conversation and conviviality with their equals.

The name of the table was purposeful. The table would bring together like-minded professionals who were committed to individualism and who used their intellect and their passions to create positive change.

Over the years, I had observed that one percent of the population had the courage to buck the status quo and move society forward. This table, which I aptly named *The One Percenters*, was not only the first women-only table but also the first specifically business-oriented one. It was my intention for the group's name to convey that we were a group of powerful innovators, the "movers and shakers," the pioneers determined to make a difference in the world. By the end of the first year, our membership had doubled.

From entering via the basement to occupying a table that commanded full attention, women at the League had made huge strides and the One Percenters were helping to lead the march.

I had come a long, long way from the rigid, male-dominated world I had grown up in.

CHAPTER 34

I WAS GROWING. I WAS THINKING. I WAS DISSATISFIED.
That's when I began to academically study the *Torah*. I started to identify the discrepancies between what was written in the Old Testament and what the rabbis had added over the next thousand years, based on their own desires and prejudices, as well as the demands of their era. I wanted to sort out the man-made laws in the Talmud from the historical laws that lie in the Old Testament. I wanted to discover the truth for myself.

I came to the passage that had changed my life forever and my heart stopped:

> *"When the Lord, your God, brings you into the land to which you are coming to possess it, he will cast away many nations from before you: the Hittites, the Girgashites, the Amorites, the Canaanites, the Perizzites, the Hivites, and the Jebusites ...seven nations more numerous and powerful than you...*
>
> *You shall not intermarry with them; you shall not give your daughter to his son, and you shall not take his daughter for your son..."*

Nowhere in the Old Testament is it forbidden to marry non-Jews per se. It's simply written, *don't marry anyone from these particular seven tribes.* If it had meant "all non-Jews," it would have used those words. *All non-Jews* was an interpretation of men added two thousand years later. John was not of those seven nations, so was the restriction on marrying him not valid?

Emboldened by my biblical studies, I also began to study the history of Jewish law. I learned, to my surprise, that the definition of Jewish birthright has been constantly shifting. Prior to the Talmudic period, the Israelites had continuous inter-marriages, and all children of mixed marriages were deemed Jewish. Then for a long stretch, children were considered Jewish only when their father was Jewish.

The Hebrew Bible provides examples of Israelite men whose children with foreign women had been accepted as Israelites. In the Middle Ages, as a response to changing societal behavior, Rabbinic law codified Jewish descent as following the maternal line exclusively. At that time paternity could be a mystery but it was always clear who a child's mother was.

Orthodox and Conservative rabbis today assert that children are Jewish only when their mother is Jewish, regardless of their paternity. Meanwhile, Reform rabbis hold to the older belief that children are Jewish when they are born to a couple in which either parent is Jewish.

And what did the Torah say on this matter? Nothing. Nowhere is the issue addressed. I was learning that Judaism is a dynamic, hybrid religion, constantly adapting to fit the times, with serious contradictions.

Consider the story of King David: Boaz, a Jewish man, died the night after his marriage to Ruth, who was not a Jewess. Some people at that time claimed that Boaz's death verified that his marriage to Ruth the Moabite had indeed been forbidden. That first night, a child was conceived.

This child's son would later become King David, the leader of the Jewish people.

Who then was a Jew?

CHAPTER 35

My MOTHER'S CANCER CAME BACK WITH A VENGEANCE. Terrified that she was dying, she implored me to come back and be part of the family again. This would require that John converts to Judaism even if it wasn't genuine. She simply wanted her daughter back while she was still alive and said that as long as John crossed the line into Judaism, my family would be accommodating to him.

As my mother battled her cancer, she waited anxiously for my reply. I called a meeting with my chosen family. John, my best friends, and their husbands gathered around me in our formal dining room, while the children played in the basement. I told them everything about my mother's wishes, her imminent death, and the choice John and I faced.

"This isn't about my conversion." John said. "This is about the life that we're willing to live and the charade that we're willing to accept in order to live it."

Maxine, the realist, weighed in. "Laya, we can talk all night, but I already know that John's not converting. So do you. Neither of you values that lifestyle."

She was right. It had taken me over 16 years to gain a strong identity and perspective. I had this amazing family right in front of me—people who supported me and loved me for myself, not for my ritualistic following of man-made rules. I still loved my parents, and I still loved my siblings, but I was happy now in my new life. It was true that I had lost respect for blind belief in religious law made by men thousands of years ago. I was going to live for myself. I had three beautiful children, a devoted husband, and a close-knit, chosen family of wonderful friends who cared about me for who I was.

"What are you thinking?" John asked.

As we mused about the impossibility of John and my leading a fundamentalist Orthodox life, I thought about a fact that my friends did not know: that so many Orthodox people do not really believe. And even if they do believe, they cut corners. They, like all humans everywhere, do what they have to do to make it work for them.

Married couples sneak TV at night, and don't follow many of the other strict, overbearing laws in the privacy of their own home. Away from home and outside the community, they indulge in food deemed non-kosher by the rabbis. They go mixed bathing and have fun at the beach while taking other liberties that stray from the letter of the law.

The highly educated members of the community nod their heads in agreement with unfounded tautologies, like creationism, but privately acknowledge that science is right.

I knew that John and I could fake it the way so many in the community do. People want more than anything to be accepted, and so will do anything necessary to stay in the community.

Would I?

I looked around the table.

"No," I said. "*We* can't have it both ways."

Relief descended over the room. At the same time, I had a heavy heart that my dear mother, my beloved siblings, and even my father were in pain. This sullied my joy as my mother's joy had been sullied.

In the months that followed, I often felt conflicted. I agonized over my choice, but I knew that I had made the right decision. John would not convert to fundamentalism. I would not give in and put the concerns of others above my family's own happiness. I would not be held responsible for anyone else's happiness. I would not live a life of deceit. I would support my chosen family the way they supported me—with the honesty and the passionate fervor of true love.

I had carried my own world upon my shoulders for so long. I shrugged.

Once it became clear that she was dying, my mother feared that the gates of heaven would close before her, if she dared embrace her independent daughter whom she so loved, and for that I never blamed her.

As my weakened, confused mother lay in bed with only days remaining, my siblings forbade me from visiting her. They told me that in her final hours, she chose not to see me. It could be true; I have no way of knowing.

My virtuous and once self-confident mother passed away at the too-early age of seventy-two.

I mourned my mother's death, but more so, the wasted years of her life. The senselessness of living in a vestibule, spending your whole life preparing for death. I mourned what could have and what should have been, our sharing in each other's lives.

I flashed back to the conundrum of my mother's words to me when I was 22 years old, still living at home and a computer programmer at MasterCard. "Laya, I wish I, too, had a satisfying career like you." Her words had taken me by complete surprise—was raising children not enough?

The weekend of my mother's death, I prepared to go to the funeral. On the morning of our departure, I received a phone call from my brother Mordechai.

"Don't come," he told me. "You're not wanted here."

I sat down at my kitchen table and tried to think through his words. It seemed likely that my mother would have also not wanted me to attend. It was probable that even in her last moments, in the name of God, she would not have wanted me there. I felt sure that all of my siblings agreed with Mordechai.

Not wanting to make a scene, I decided not to force myself upon them. Reluctantly, as I gave my loyal friends the news, we sat together in my living room in disbelief. It was a small, private mourning, both for the death of my mother and the chance of ever fulfilling her hopes for me. As always, my chosen family helped me survive yet another rejection.

Many years later, when I confronted my brother about this unforgiving and heartbreaking exclusion, he simply said, "You should not have listened to me. Why didn't you just come?"

The week following my mother's passing was particularly difficult. When someone dies, Jewish tradition mandates observance of *Shiva* for seven days. This is a time of mourning, prayer, and reflection. The world stops, and all thoughts are on the dearly departed. Preventing me from being allowed at the funeral was one matter, but not attending the *Shiva* was another level of cruelty. My siblings banned me from the house I had once called home. So, I grieved without them. Months later, I received a letter containing my mother's will.

'....*I make no provision for my daughter, Laya Steinberg. In no event shall she be entitled to receive any part of my estate pursuant to the provisions of this Will or as an intestate distribution.*"

I stood in the front hallway of my home and read it again: *I make no provision for my daughter, Laya Steinberg.* I had no idea of the worth of my mother's valuables nor what she had accumulated and left in her will, but it held no importance to me.

I signed the documents and affirmed my mother's last wish. I wanted no part of her estate.

My father was born in northern Israel, in the city of *Tzvat* (Safad), and in a way, he never really left it. All of his formative experiences had happened there. Now, Israel was also home to hundreds of relatives, including my sister Syrle and my brother Mordechai, who was the dean of the Slonimer Yeshiva. My father wanted to die in the Holy Land and be buried on Mount Olive, the sanctified burial place for the most devout. Eventually, both he and my mother were laid to rest there.

On one of my father's many trips to Israel, he had a heart attack. His doctor admitted him to the hospital and the surgeons immediately performed triple bypass surgery. Candice called me to report the terrifying news. I had not seen my father in ten years and feared that this might be his end. I immediately boarded a plane to Israel to say goodbye.

I arrived at the King David Hotel, where I quickly changed into a long skirt, making sure I was modestly dressed according to

Rabbinic laws. I left my head uncovered. Only married women were required to wear wigs, and for once, I was glad that my family didn't consider me married.

During the ride, I held tight to my positive expectations. *I'm sure he'll be happy to see me but what will he say? What will I say? Was it right to come here, or am I foolishly hoping for what I know is impossible?*

I arrived at the hospital.

His room was sterile and cold.

"Laya," he called as I walked toward him. "You're here! Come closer."

I was relieved that he seemed glad to see me.

"Stand next to my left ear so I can hear you. I can't hear in the right." His weak, shaking hands pulled me closer to him. I tried not to look at the tubes covering his body and the monitors attached to his arms and chest.

"Yes, Dad. I'm here."

"See what happened to me?" he asked in dismay. "Are you repenting and coming back to God and the family? Is that why you came? It's about time. Something terrible will happen if you do not leave that no-goodnik. You are not married, and your children will suffer in the years to come."

I flinched at his cruel words. How quickly the reprimands came. My hopes had been, as always, foolish. Deep down, I knew even before I stepped off the plane that I was going to receive a lecture. I had been kidding myself. But also, I knew that I could bear it. I did what I always did, listened silently. *It will be over soon enough. Hold on until the scolding is over. You're doing the right thing by being here by your father's side, no matter what he says.*

"You're wasting your life," he ranted. "What are you doing to your children? They will be lost with a dismal future. They will be lost." He put special emphasis on the ills that would befall my children because they grew up in a home where their father was not Jewish. His frenzy grew as he raged on and on, causing the tubes and wires that were attached to him to become displaced.

"What now?" asked a nurse who had rushed in to find out what the commotion was all about. Apparently, this was not the first burst of hysterics from my father. She rearranged the tubes, and left, unperturbed that her patient was just in another one of his rages.

I continued to stand and listen. This is not what I had come to Israel to hear. In retrospect, I should not have allowed the abuse to go on, but then again, my parents had taught me to be an obedient daughter.

When my siblings and I were growing up and my father walked into the room, we would all stand up and not speak until addressed. We strictly followed the commandment to honor thy father and thy mother. My parents raised us in that world, and many aspects of my upbringing have stayed with me.

That afternoon, Mordechai arrived at the hospital in his Hasidic garb. He nodded awkwardly to acknowledge me. I knew that he loved me and was glad to see me, but he didn't know what to do. Although he was civil, it was difficult for both of us.

What were the rebbe's instructions? Was he allowed to talk to me? I knew he was acting under a decree from the authority above. He wasn't allowed to trust his own instincts.

Years earlier during his visit to the US, Mordechai had taken a cab to my house to discuss religious principles, hoping that he could get me to rejoin the family and the faith.

"I'm not religious, Mordechai. I have lost my belief in religion."

He stood there, stiff and tense. When he realized that I truly had no interest, he simply said, "So there is nothing I can do to change your mind?"

"There isn't."

"Okay, so I'll get going." *Just like that?* He walked out the door, got into the waiting taxi, and left.

We hadn't seen each other for twelve long years. My brother! Did I not mean anything to him at all? My heart sank. I so much yearned for him to stay and talk to me, spend time with me and to reminisce about those nostalgic youthful years we had enjoyed as children. Didn't he miss me? …. I had known on my way to Reno 25 years ago, *(as I was about to marry the forbidden, they would write me off….).* I was right.

From that day forward, he stopped his ritual of sending me his hand-baked matzah from Israel for Passover. The yearly birthday cards he used to send ceased as well. I wondered how he could so easily abandon me.

My sister Syrle was the next to arrive. The moment she stepped into the room, she deliberately turned her back on me. She would not face me. Had she known I was going to be there she would never have come. I tried not to show my disbelief. I did not want anyone else to feel uncomfortable. I took in her tall frame, straight as an arrow, the kerchief over her head, the long dress covering her legs, and her stern, unyielding profile.

Still, beneath it all, I knew she yearned to connect with me the way I yearned to connect with her.

We were visiting on a Friday, and before the Sabbath began at sundown the nurses set up a table and chairs for our Sabbath dinner in the corner of the hospital room.

Syrle observed the seating carefully. When I sat across the table from her, she pointedly stood up and swung her chair around. I sat there stunned and misplaced, staring at the broad expanse of her back. Was she trying to punish me, or insult me, or was she simply denying my existence? I set my napkin on my lap and struggled to hide the hot flush of shock and humiliation rising to my face. *Could this be an order from her husband?*

In Judaism, if you abandon your faith, your family could sit *Shiva* for you. In my situation, because I was still Jewish and my children were Jewish I was not dead, yet Syrle treated me as though I should be.

The evening was very painful, but confronting her was out of the question. My brother spoke to me, my father lectured me, and other relatives interacted with me, but as far as Syrle was concerned, I was nonexistent. She would not look at my face, endeavoring to make me disappear. She kept up this behavior the entire evening.

I was stunned, and to this day have never been able to erase the scene from my memory. The only way I managed to bear the hurt was to remind myself that my visit was not about me, it was about my father and his well-being.

As I sat there, unable to eat or drink, I tried to see the situation from her point of view. In her mind, the *Almighty God* would want it this way, because I was sinning. Therefore, she was forbidden to acknowledge my existence or do anything but shun me into repentance. As far as she was concerned, I was not worthy of existence in my state of sin. When Syrle turned away from me it was an awful act, but I understood that it was her religious duty and did not begrudge her.

Even though I understood their motivations, the evening was a complete nightmare. I made a promise to myself, *Don't sacrifice—do not allow anyone to force you into that miserable position, ever again.*

Back in my hotel room, it was particularly upsetting that my father had threatened: *harm may befall your children as a punishment for your sins.* I would not allow anyone to plant such thoughts in my head. Wouldn't every parent who loves their children feel the same?

Finally, I called my husband and two girlfriends to help me stay grounded. It was a relief to talk to them. My double dose of unpleasantness—my father's badgering and my sister's ostracism—prompted me to cut the visit short. I returned home as soon as I could.

By the following week, my father had had enough of the entire hospital scene. He pulled out his IVs and stormed out of the hospital. I pictured him in his white hospital gown, bearded, barefoot, and furious, righteously storming down the streets of Jerusalem like a modern-day prophet, determined to have the last word, and determined that the world would forever bend to his impervious will.

I would not. I was no longer a child.

I thought back to the father I had looked up to as a little girl. When he was younger, he had shed his *pe'us*, participated in the mainstream business world, and embraced the American values of freedom and individuality. In doing so, he had enjoyed enormous success as a global importer and exporter of textiles. But over the years of wondering if he was becoming too secular, and after enduring the ups and downs of business and other vicissitudes of life, his self-confidence in his past choices had waned.

I remembered an astonishing moment from one of my visits home, years earlier. My father had looked at me quite pointedly and said, "I admire your independence." It was a remarkable admission that he held my accomplishments in high regard.

What had happened to his own independence? His own self-confidence?

When I left, he was utterly crushed. Whereas before he had based his identity on his scholarship, his business accomplishments, and his raising of six holy and respected children. After my elopement none of that mattered. In his mind, everything was tainted by this failure. How could something like this have happened? Why had he let me take a job in the secular world? Had he made an arrogant mistake in moving to Long Island and trying to build his own Orthodox community, instead of staying with the existing community in The Lower East Side of Manhattan?

I was eleven, doing my homework with my sisters when a flash of lightning jolted us to attention. In unison, we jumped out of our chairs and rushed into the living room, grasping the draperies and lifting them for an unobstructed view of the outside. We peered through the windows in anticipation.

The thunder startled us, even though we knew it was coming. We quickly said the blessing for thunder together: *Blessed are You, God, King of the universe, for Your strength and power fill the world.* We huddled under the curtains, glued to the window, waiting for another bolt of lightning.

"I see the lightning," Candice cried as a blinding, crooked beam seared itself onto our retinas. We waited for the terrific boom that shook the windows and confirmed what we had seen and said the blessing for the lightning: *Blessed are You, God, King of the universe, Who makes the works of creation.*

Like most children, I was afraid of thunder and lightning. I was told that God created them as a warning, to remind us of his power. *Could God punish us?* I asked myself. *I haven't sinned, but we're all responsible for all Jews. God might punish us for sins that other Jews committed. God might send an earthquake and the earth will gobble us up. He might strike us down with a bolt of lightning.*

The blessings we said gave me temporary comfort that God and I were on the same side. It was reassuring that God could and would make everything okay, even if He was sending terrifying explosions through the sky. There was a reason for the lightning, and we put everything in God's hands and trusted it was for the best.

A month after his hospital revolt, while my father lay dying in his hospital bed, as an act of penitence and in search of comfort, his mind receded back into the safety of his childhood, his *cha'dar,* and in the *shtetl* of his grandfather, as well as the superstitions embedded in his faith, which had guided his life.

No lightning bolt would illuminate him, or thunderclaps wake him to a new understanding.

I knew that deep down he loved me, but he was too afraid to show it. He could not relent.

My own choice was to walk from the dark, into the light. The sacrifices would weigh heavily on me, but in moments when the burden seems too much, I am sustained by my father's whispered words from long ago.

Laya, I admire your independence...

And so I go forward. Always toward the light.

EPILOGUE

"It is not an escape from suffering that we should seek,
but rather a quest for joy."

DESPITE EVERYTHING THAT OCCURRED, MY FAMILY
members are actually warmhearted, kind, and intelligent
people. They are always surrounded by books. They can discuss
history, philosophy, culture, and Jewish theology.

Yet with all their learning and potential for independent
thought, they are clannish and exclusive. They realize that a
non-Jewish world exists around them, but it is simply not their
world. They feel that the outside world is inferior to theirs, and
this influences everything they say or do.

My family retreated into a Jewish enclave that became ever
tighter and more parochial. All the beauty and secular culture
my parents once enjoyed no longer held importance in their
lives. In many ways, they may as well have lived the last part of
their lives in the Warsaw ghetto of 200 years ago.

To an outsider, such behavior can seem astonishing. To me,
it was just sad.

I knew exactly why Syrle turned away from me in my
father's hospital room. I did not begrudge her for it. In her
belief system and her faith, she proceeded as she did because
God told her to do so. She was not acting on her own; she was
acting in the name of God.

This particular behavior, as the world well knows, is not restricted to Orthodox Jews. There are fundamentalists, radicals, and zealots in every religion. They do a tremendous amount of harm to society as a whole and to the individuals who dare to push against their accepted ways.

I say a silent prayer to my mother: *I am sorry.*

Not sorry that I left the fold, but sorry that she missed out on sharing in my life and the lives of my children.

My story does not end here. Over the coming years, my life took more twists and turns. Eleven years after the death of my father I danced at the first of my children's weddings, and soon after that, grandchildren began to arrive and my life was rich with family and love. My children have so far given me five grandchildren. Within my *family by choice*, there are four more.

Looking back on this story, I have no regrets in following my heart and choosing my own life's path. Escaping the cocoon of Fundamentalist Judaism and emerging from my deep-seated indoctrination was a long and difficult process, but it made me the person I am today.

The fundamentalists have recently shed their fear of college education for girls. They have come to realize that it's a requirement for financial success and the easier life that wealth can bring. It's self-serving, keeping the younger generations in the fold. Nevertheless, women are still viewed as the *'ezer kenegdo'* (a helper for man as written in Genesis). The humiliation of the Mikvah still stands, keeping the women intact.

The power of indoctrination breeds non-thinking, non-questioning, and absurdity.... just believing that coins fall from the sky.

When I witnessed the wrongs of the world growing up, I wanted to make this world a better place. I wanted to heal the pain of life's disappointments. I wanted to fulfill my desires for freedom and unfettered achievement and to raise children to carry that same hopeful vision forward. The world ought to be a wonderful, happy, fulfilling place where people can live and work without fear. My hope is that this story will serve as an example that it *is* possible to create a life of one's own choosing.

If I have touched the heart of one person, it was worth it. Anyone who feels trapped in a family that says *no*, let me rekindle your spirit and assure you—you can have a family that says *yes*.

MY STORY IN PHOTOGRAPHS

Last Visit with Dad in Israel

My visit to Slonim, Belarus 2011

Ancestor's Shtetle

Great Great Grandfather

My father and his sister's journey
to USA

My father as a young man

My mother's graduation

PHOTOGRAPHS

My parents' wedding

Father at house in Long Island

Cousin Shani and Aunt Esther

Left to Right (Uncle, Father,
Mother, Paternal Grandmother)

Young Rita at 5 years old (Laya)

My High School Graduation

Summer after marriage

Rita in 4th Grade
(2nd row 3rd from left)

Mother and I

Move to Philadelphia

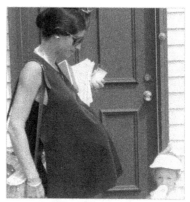

Twins on the way

My baby daughter and I

Career Mom

My daughter and I

PHOTOGRAPHS

Our House

John and Children

Nonna and Children

Shani and Children

Our young family

John and Laya Sailing

Sailing at Center Island, NY

John and the Twins sailing on Poseidon

My twins and Michael at camp

Laya and John at Nonnas

My daughter's Bat Mitzvah

Family by choice at Bat Mitzvah

Laya Birthday Dinner with Family by Choice

My Teenage Children

My Young Children

My Youngest Twin

My daughter and I in Spain

My Eldest Twin

One Percenters Club Table
at The Union League of Philadelphia

Union League Friends

Our boat, Poseidon   MVP after all of these years

My first grandchild

My Eldest Granddaughter

Trish and I with our first grandchildren

Grandchildren at the beach house

ACKNOWLEDGMENTS

I AM FOREVER GRATEFUL TO THE MEMBERS OF MY *FAMILY of Choice*: Trish, John, Ashley, Maxine, Jeff, Michael, Tamie, Mark, Denise, Gila and Gadi, Orpaz, Gilad; to Shawn Kent, Connie Aramaki, Maya Kalieva, and Chad Hopenwasser; and to Robert Finkel, for exposing me to the work of Ayn Rand. I cherish them and they have cherished me in return. This family gave me unconditional love and shared times of joy, pain, triumph, heartache, and extraordinary fun. They have been a constant source of happiness in my life.

I am filled with gratitude to my husband Gary for his unwavering support and encouragement as I worked on this project. His patience was without limit and it made this journey into my past possible.

I have immense gratitude to my editor Diana Holquist, who put her heart into my memoir. She guided me with love and patience and helped me to sort my emotions, bring out the innocence of my youth, formulate my thoughts, and capture real-life moments. Thank you also to my assistants, Kiera Evans, Gina Purri, and Dalla Andracchio, who gave me significant insight and advice that greatly improved the final versions. And to Alan Roth, my final editor, who believed in me and shared my passion to bring this memoir out to the world.

Finally, I am fortunate for my eternal love to my children Michelle, Seth, and Zachary; to my adored grandchildren; and to Della, Francis and Rachel. I am forever grateful to my first husband John; for loving me, having the courage to marry me, and showing me a world I never knew existed. He gave me the courage to become the person I am.

ABOUT THE AUTHOR

LAYA WAS RAISED IN A traditional Orthodox home and was destined to become a housewife until her life took an unexpected turn. After initially studying at Yeshiva University, she began working during the infancy of computers, climbing the industry's ranks to become one of MasterCard's first female programmers. Laya went on to found two successful data processing companies serving Fortune 500 clients and was identified by the *Philadelphia Business Journal* as one of Philadelphia's Top 25 Women Business Owners. She is credited with founding the first female club (and business club) table at the Union League of Philadelphia.

Laya has three grown children and works in the Philadelphia suburbs where she resides with her second husband. As two-time president of her local Rotary Club and a Paul Harris fellow, she regularly engages in international community service projects. When not writing, speaking, or spending time with her grandchildren, she travels extensively throughout the world.

Her next project will be the creation of a secular cultural center called, "The Cultural Center For Virtue." The Center will be a warm and loving place that accepts and finds value in each person. It will be a space for families and individuals to be embraced by a community and to participate in lessons and events, with no religious affiliation. This will build a community of character that endures from generation to generation.

Email: **Author.Laya@gmail.com**   Website: **AuthorLaya.com**

HEBREW GLOSSARY

Alef bais: The Hebrew Alphabet

Alef: The first letter of the Hebrew Alphabet 'A'

Asher Yatzar: A silent Jewish prayer said after leaving the bathroom

Ay-shet Cha-yil: A woman of valor

Baal Koreh: The Torah reader

Bat Mitzvah: The terms **bar mitzvah** *(Hebrew:* רַב מֶצְוָהַ) and **bat mitzvah** (Hebrew: תַ מֶצְוָהַ; Ashkenazi pronunciation: "bas mitzvah") refer to the coming-of-age ritual in Judaism; "bar" is used for a boy, while "bat" is used for a girl. According to Jewish law, before children reach a certain age, the parents are said to "become" a bar or bat mitzvah, at which point they begin to be held accountable for their own actions. (Traditionally, the father of a bar or bat mitzvah offers thanks to God that he is no longer punished for his child's sins)

Beth Jacob: Hebrew word for the House of Jacob (Father of the 10 tribes of Israel)

Bimah: The altar part and podium in the sanctuary where the Torah is read in Jewish Synagogues

Cha'dar: Jewish kindergarten for little boys

Challah: Challah is a special bread of Ashkenazi Jewish origin, usually braided and typically eaten on ceremonial occasions such as Shabbos and major Jewish holidays

Eretz Yisroel: Hebrew word for The Land of Israel

Ezer kenegdo: The literal meaning is a helper of man as written in Genesis. Referred to Eve being created to be Adam's helper. God said that man needs someone by his side, in order to live on earth. Hebrew phrase וְדָגָנְכ רֶעַ, in Genesis 2:18

Gehenna: Also referred to as *Gehinnom,* which means "burning in hell"

Get: A *Get* is the religious version of a civil divorce. Without that document, women are not free to remarry

Hallaf: A razor-sharp, polished knife

Hametz: Leavened bread, which is forbidden to be eaten, or even have in a Jewish household on Passover

Hashem: Hebrew word for God

Hasidism: The different schools, or interpretations, of Hasidism, are known as dynasties. They were often named after the town in which they started. Out of Slonim came Slonimer Hasidism. It was a more scholarly form of Hasidic Judaism formed to shift the focus away from glorified mysticism and back toward the idea that studying the *Talmud* was the greatest good

Kabbalah: The mystical branch of Judaism

Kapparot: On the eve of Yom Kippur, Kapparot involves swinging a living chicken three times around your head, while reciting a prayer. Traditionally, men use roosters and women hens. After the ceremony, the animal is slaughtered, as a sacrifice, according to Jewish law

Kiddush: The blessing on the wine in a melodic tone

Kollel: A yeshiva for married men

Kosher or Kashrus: A set of dietary laws dealing with the foods that Jews are permitted to eat and how those foods must be prepared according to Jewish law

Kugel: Kugel is a baked pudding or casserole, most commonly made from Jewish egg noodles or potatoes. It is a traditional Ashkenazi Jewish dish, often served on Shabbos and Jewish holidays

Matzah: Matzah is unleavened bread that is part of Jewish cuisine and forms an integral element of the Passover festival, during which *hametz* is forbidden

Mazel tov: Congratulations

Meshulach: Singular for *Meshulachim*

Meshulachim: Jewish beggars, called *meshulachim* (messengers of charity)

Mikvah: Ritual bath for married women, to officially cleanse herself after her Period is over and after she counts seven clean days. She is then allowed to have intercourse with her husband

Minyan: In Judaism, the minimum number of males (10) is required to constitute a representative "community of Israel" for liturgical purposes. A Jewish boy at least the age of 13 may form part of the quorum after his Bar Mitzvah (religious adulthood)

Modeh Ani: Jewish Morning Prayer to God giving thanks for being alive

Negel vasser: Jewish morning ritual of washing your hands is the first thing you do in the bathroom before doing anything else

Pe'us or pe'ot: Hebrew term for **sidelocks or sideburns.** Payot is worn by some men and boys in the Orthodox Jewish community based on an interpretation of the Hebrew Bible injunction against shaving the "sides" of one's head. Literally, pe'ah means "corner, side, edge." *pe'ot,* plural: תוֹאֵפ

Rebbe: At the head of every dynasty is the *rebbe.* Unlike a Rabbi, who is respected in his particular congregation, the *rebbe* is a supreme leader revered by everyone in the community; he is a holy man who is regarded as the community's link to God himself

Rosh Hashanah: The Jewish New Year holiday, ten days prior to *Yom Kippur*

Rugelach: Rugelach is a filled baked confection originating in the Jewish communities of Poland. It is popular in Israel, and commonly found in most cafes and bakeries

Shabbos: This day is the Jewish Sabbath. For the Orthodox Jews, it is a day of rest without any work performed on that day

Sheitel: A wig that every Fundamentalist Jewish married woman wears to cover her hair, so as not to be attractive to another man other than her husband

Shtetl: A small Jewish town or village in eastern Europe; a small plain room where very pious men sit and study the Talmud every day

Siddur: Hebrew Jewish prayer book

Shadchan: A matchmaker is usually a professional individual who arranges a date between a single boy and a single girl. The matchmaker vets both of them prior to the date to determine if they are a suitable match

Shadchanim: Plural for *Shadchan*

Shidduch: An ancient matchmaking tradition among Orthodox singles

Shiva: Mourning the deceased for seven days; wearing the same clothes, sitting on wooden chairs, and not attending to any business or personal affairs

Shochet: The professional who slaughters animals and birds according to strict Torah laws that deem them kosher

Tachlis: Hebrew word for "purpose"; girls and boys go out on dates, for 'purpose' rather than date for fun

Talmud: The body of Jewish civil and ceremonial law and legend comprising the writings and laws of the Mishnah and the Gemara. There are two versions of the Talmud: the *Babylonian Talmud* (which dates from the 5th century AD but includes earlier material) and the earlier *Palestinian or Jerusalem Talmud*

Talmid Chacham: Torah scholar

Tatty: Father in Yiddish

Tishah B'av: The ninth day of the Hebrew month of *Av, (usually in the month of July)* This is a day of mourning and remembrance of the destruction of the Temple in Israel, first by the Babylonians and then by the Romans in 70 of AD

Tref: Forbidden food for Jewish people. Not Kosher.

Tzitzits: Tzitzits are specially knotted ritual fringes, or tassels, worn in antiquity by Israelites and today by observant Jews

Tzvat: Safad is a city in the North of Israel

Yarmulke: Yiddish word for The Jewish head covering for a male. Also called *Kippah* in Hebrew

Yeshiva: A religious school for males

Yichus: Fine Pedigree

Yiddish: A language used by Jewish people in central and eastern Europe before the Holocaust. It was originally a German dialect with words from Hebrew and several modern languages and is today spoken mainly in the US, Israel, and Russia

Yom Kippur: The Day of Atonement, which is the most sacred day of the year for the Jewish People

Printed in the USA
CPSIA information can be obtained
at www.ICGtesting.com
LVHW091229041123
762992LV00003B/258